On the H

St. Ambrose of Milan

Edited by Paul A. Böer, Sr.

VERITATIS SPLENDOR PUBLICATIONS
et cognoscetis veritatem et veritas liberabit vos (Jn 8:32)

MMXIV

Cover Art
VIVARINI, Bartolomeo
St Ambrose Polyptych (detail)
1477
Tempera on wood
Gallerie dell'Accademia, Venice

The text of this book is excerpted from:

A Select Library of the Nicene and Post-Nicene Fathers of the Christian Church, ed. Philip Schaff, LL.D. (Buffalo: The Christian Literature Co., 1887). Vol. X Ambrose: Select Works and Letters.

The text of this work is in the public domain.

Retypeset and republished in 2014 by Veritatis Splendor Publications.

AD MAJOREM DEI GLORIAM

A SELECT LIBRARY
OF THE
NICENE AND
POST-NICENE FATHERS
OF
THE CHRISTIAN CHURCH.
SECOND SERIES

**TRANSLATED INTO ENGLISH WITH PROLEGOMENA AND
EXPLANATORY NOTES.**

Edited by

PHILIP SCHAFF, D.D., LL.D.,
PROFESSOR OF CHURCH HISTORY IN THE UNION
THEOLOGICAL SEMINARY, NEW YORK.

AND

HENRY WACE, D.D.,
PRINCIPAL OF KING'S COLLEGE, LONDON.

VOLUME X
Ambrose: Select Works and Letters

T&T CLARK
EDINBURGH

WM. B. EERDMANS PUBLISHING COMPANY
GRAND RAPIDS, MICHIGAN

SOME OF
THE PRINCIPAL WORKS OF ST. AMBROSE,
TRANSLATED
BY
THE REV. H. DE ROMESTIN, M.A.
OF ST. JOHN'S COLLEGE, AND RECTOR OF TIPTREE, ESSEX,
WITH THE ASSISTANCE OF
THE REV. E. DE ROMESTIN, M.A.
OF NEW COLLEGE, OXFORD,
AND
THE REV. H. T. F. DUCKWORTH, M.A.
OF MERTON COLLEGE, OXFORD.

Introduction to the Three Books of St. Ambrose on the Holy Spirit.

The three books on the Holy Spirit are, as St. Ambrose says himself, a sequel to those on the Faith, and the two treatises together have been sometimes quoted as if one, with the title, De Trinitate. But we see from Gratian's letter to St. Ambrose, and from the reply, that each treatise is separate, and the De Spiritu Sancto was written some years later, a.d. 381.

In the first book St. Ambrose commences by allegorizing the history of Gideon and the fleece, seeing in the drying of the fleece and the moistening of the threshing-floor a type of the Holy Spirit leaving the Jews and being poured out on the Gentiles. Passing to his more immediate subject, he proves that the Holy Spirit is above the whole Creation and is truly God, alleging as a special argument that the sin against the Holy Spirit can never be forgiven, here or hereafter. He shows how the Holy Spirit is in Scripture called the Spirit of God; that He spake by the prophets and apostles; that He sanctifies men, and is typified by the mystical ointment spoken of in Scripture. Next, St. Ambrose treats of His oneness with the other two Persons of the Holy Trinity, and shows that His mission in no way detracts from this oneness, but that there is in all the Divine Persons a perfect unity of peace, love, and other virtues.

The second book commences with a treatment of the history of Samson in the same way as that of Gideon in Book I. Samson always succeeded so long as the Holy Spirit was with him, but fell into misfortune so soon as he was forsaken. It is shown that the power of the Holy Spirit is the same as that of the Father and the Son, and that there is an agreement in design and working, and in vivifying man. He is Creator and therefore to be worshipped, and He worked with the Father and the Son in founding the Church, and in conclusion is proved the unity of operation in the Three Persons.

The third book continues the same argument, showing that the mission of prophets and apostles, and even of the Son Himself, is to be referred to the Spirit, yet without any subjection on the part of the Son, seeing that the Spirit also receives His mission from the Father and the Son. The Godhead of the Holy Spirit is next taken up and proved, when occasion is taken also to show that there are not three Gods or three Lords, for the Three Divine Persons are one in holiness and nature; and the work is concluded with a summary of some of the principal arguments.

There can be but little doubt that this is the work, and St. Ambrose the author, bitterly attacked by St. Jerome; the whole passage may be read in the Apology of Rufinus, p. 470, in vol. iii. of this series. St. Ambrose is compared to a daw decked in another bird's plumage, and charged with writing "bad things in Latin taken from good things in Greek," and St. Jerome even took the trouble to translate a work of St. Didymus on the Holy Spirit (from the preface to which the above extracts are taken), in order that those who did not know Greek might, St. Jerome hoped, recognize the plagiarisms.

Rufinus vigorously defends St. Ambrose, and, pointing out many inconsistencies in his opponent, says: "The saintly Ambrose wrote his book on the Holy Spirit not in words only but with his own blood, for he offered his life-blood to his persecutors, and shed it within himself, though God preserved his life for future labours." [781]

The truth is that St. Ambrose being a good Greek scholar, and having undertaken to write on the Holy Spirit, studied what others had written before him, and made use of what had been urged by SS. Basil, Didymus, and others. The opinion of the great St. Augustine concerning this treatise may be set against that of St. Jerome. "St. Ambrose when treating of the deep subject of the Holy Spirit, and showing that He is equal with the Father and the Son, yet makes use of a simple style of discourse; inasmuch as his subject required no the embellishments of language, but proofs to move the minds of his readers." [782]

[781] See vol. iii. p. 471, of this series.

[782] De doct. Christ. IV. c. 21.

CONTENTS

Chapter I. St. Ambrose commences his argument by complimenting the Emperor, both for his faith and for the restitution of the Basilica to the Church; then having urged that his opponents, if they affirm that the Holy Spirit is not a servant, cannot deny Him to be above all, adds that the same Spirit, when He said, "All things serve Thee," showed plainly that He was distinct from creatures; which point he also establishes by other evidence. 37

Chapter II. The words, "All things were made by Him," are not a proof that the Holy Spirit is included amongst all things, since He was not made. For otherwise it could be proved by other passages that the Son, and even the Father Himself, must be numbered amongst all things, which would be similar irreverence. 39

Chapter III. The statement of the Apostle, that all things are of the Father by the Son, does not separate the Spirit from Their company, since what is referred to one Person is also attributed to each. So those baptized in the Name of Christ are held to be baptized in the Name of the Father and of the Holy Spirit, if, that is, there is belief in the Three Persons, otherwise the baptism will be null. This also applies to baptism in the Name of the Holy Spirit. If because of one passage the Holy Spirit is separated from the Father and the Son, it will necessarily follow from other passages that the Father will be subordinated to the Son. The Son is worshipped by angels, not by the Spirit, for the latter is His witness, not His servant. Where the Son is spoken of as being before all, it is to be understood of creatures. The great dignity of the Holy Spirit is proved by the absence of forgiveness for the sin against Him. How it is that such sin cannot be forgiven, and how the Spirit is one.

Chapter IV. The Holy Spirit is one and the same Who spake in the prophets and apostles, Who is the Spirit of God and of Christ; Whom, further, Scripture designates the Paraclete, and the Spirit of life and truth

Chapter V. The Holy Spirit, since He sanctifies creatures, is neither a creature nor subject to change. He is always good, since He is given by the Father and the Son; neither is He to be numbered amongst such things as are said to fail. He must be acknowledged as the source of goodness. The Spirit of God's mouth, the amender of evils, and Himself good. Lastly, as He is said in Scripture to be good, and is joined to the Father and the Son in baptism, He cannot possibly be denied to be good. He is not, however, said to progress, but to be made perfect in goodness, which distinguishes Him from all creatures.

Chapter VI. Although we are baptized with water and the Spirit, the latter is much superior to the former, and is not therefore to be separated from the Father and the Son.

Chapter VII. The Holy Spirit is not a creature, seeing that He is infinite, and was shed upon the apostles dispersed through all countries, and moreover sanctifies the Angels also, to whom He makes us equal. Mary was full of the same likewise, so too, Christ the Lord, and so far all things

utterances, and by Spirit is signified the human soul as also the flesh assumed by Christ. And since this was created by each Person of the Trinity, it is thence argued that the Spirit, Who has before been affirmed to be the Creator of all things, was the Author of the Incarnation of the Lord.

shows that the Spirit called the Church exactly as the Father and the Son did, and proves this by the selection of SS. Paul and Barnabas, and especially by the mission of St. Peter to Cornelius. And by the way he points out how in the Apostle's vision the calling of the Gentiles was shadowed forth, who having been before like wild beasts, now by the operation of the Spirit lay aside that wildness. Then having quoted other passages in support of this view, he shows that in the case of Jeremiah cast into a pit by Jews, and rescued by Abdemelech, is a type of the slighting of the Holy Spirit by the Jews, and of His being honoured by the Gentiles.

Chapter XI. We shall follow the example of Abdemelech, if we believe that the Son and Holy Spirit know all things. This knowledge is attributed in Scripture to the Spirit, and also to the Son. The Son is glorified by the Spirit, as also the Spirit by the Son. Also, inasmuch as we read that the Father, the Son, and the Spirit say and reveal the same things, we must acknowledge in Them a oneness of nature and knowledge. Lastly, that the Spirit searcheth the deep things of God is not a mark of ignorance, since the Father and the Son are likewise said to search, and Paul, although chosen by Christ, yet was taught by the Spirit.

Chapter XII. After proof that the Spirit is the Giver of revelation equally with the Father and the Son, it is explained how the same Spirit does not speak of Himself; and it is shown that no bodily organs are to be thought of in Him, and that no inferiority is to be supposed from the fact of our reading that He hears, since the same would have to be attributed to the Son, and indeed even to the Father, since He hears the Son. The Spirit then hears and

Chapter XVI. The Father is holy, and likewise the Son and
the Spirit, and so They are honoured in the same
Trisagion: nor can we speak more worthily of God than
by calling Him Holy; whence it is clear that we must not
derogate from the dignity of the Holy Spirit. In Him is all
which pertains to God, since in baptism He is named with

Three Books of St. Ambrose, Bishop of Milan, on the Holy Spirit.

To the Emperor Gratian.

Book I.

The choice of Gideon was a figure of our Lord's Incarnation, the sacrifice of a kid, of the satisfaction for sins in the body of Christ; that of the bullock, of the abolition of profane rites; and in the three hundred soldiers was a type of the future redemption through the cross. The seeking of various signs by Gideon was also a mystery, for by the dryness and moistening of the fleece was signified the falling away of the Jews and the calling of the Gentiles, by the water received in a basin the washing of the apostles' feet. St. Ambrose prays that his own pollution may be washed away, and praises the loving-kindness of Christ. The same water sent forth by the Son of God effects marvellous conversions; it cannot, however, be sent by any other, since it is the pouring forth of the Holy Spirit, Who is subject to no external power.

1. When Jerubbaal, as we read, was beating out wheat [783] under an oak, he received a message from God in order that he might bring the people of God from the power of strangers into liberty. Nor is it a matter of wonder if he was chosen for grace, seeing that even then, being appointed under the shadow of the holy cross and of the adorable Wisdom in the predestined mystery of the future Incarnation, he was bringing forth the visible grains of the fruitful corn from their hiding places, and was [mystically] separating the elect of the saints from the refuse of the empty chaff. For these elect, as though

27

trained with the rod of truth, laying aside the superfluities of the old man together with his deeds, are gathered in the Church as in a winepress. For the Church is the winepress of the eternal fountain, since from her wells forth the juice of the heavenly Vine.

2. And Gideon, moved by that message, when he heard that, though thousands of the people failed, God would deliver His own from their enemies by means of one man, [784] offered a kid, and according to the word of the Angel, laid its flesh and the unleavened cakes upon the rock, and poured the broth upon them. And as soon as the Angel touched them with the end of the staff which he bore, fire burst forth out of the rock, and so the sacrifice which he was offering was consumed. [785] By which it seems clear that that rock was a figure of the Body of Christ, for it is written: "They drank of that rock that followed them, and that rock was Christ." [786] Which certainly refers not to His Godhead, but to His Flesh, which watered the hearts of the thirsting people with the perpetual stream of His Blood.

3. Even at that time was it declared in a mystery that the Lord Jesus in His Flesh would, when crucified, do away the sins of the whole world, and not only the deeds of the body, but the desires of the soul. For the flesh of the kid refers to sins of deed, the broth to the enticements of desire as it is written: "For the people lusted an evil lust, and said, Who shall give us flesh to eat?" [787] That the Angel then stretched forth his staff, and touched the rock, from which fire went out, [788] shows that the Flesh of the Lord, being filled with the Divine Spirit, would burn away all the sins of human frailty. Wherefore, also, the Lord says: "I am come to send fire upon the earth." [789]

4. Then the man, instructed and foreknowing what was to be, observes the heavenly mysteries, and therefore, according to the warning, slew the bullock destined by his father to idols, and himself offered to God another bullock seven years old. [790] By doing which he most plainly showed that after the coming of the Lord all Gentile sacrifices should be done away, and that only the sacrifice of the Lord's passion should be offered for the redemption of the people. For that bullock was, in a type, Christ, in Whom, as Esaias said, dwelt the fulness of the seven gifts of the Spirit. [791] This bullock Abraham also offered when he saw the day of the Lord and was glad. [792] He it is Who was offered at one time in the type of a kid, at another in that of a sheep, at another in that of a bullock. Of a kid, because He is a sacrifice for sin; of a sheep, because He is an unresisting victim; of a bullock, because He is a victim without blemish.

5. Holy Gideon then saw the mystery beforehand. Next he chose out three hundred for the battle, so as to show that the world should be freed from the incursion of worse enemies, not by the multitude of their number, but by the mystery of the cross. And yet, though he was brave and faithful, he asked of the Lord yet fuller proofs of future victory, saying: "If Thou wilt save Israel by mine hand, O Lord, as Thou hast said, behold I will put a fleece of wool on the threshing-floor, and if there shall be dew on the fleece and dryness on all the ground, I shall know that Thou wilt deliver the people by my hand according to Thy promise. And it was so." [793] Afterwards he asked in addition that dew should descend on all the earth and dryness be on the fleece.

6. Some one perhaps will enquire whether he does not seem to have been wanting in faith, seeing that after being instructed by

many signs he asked still more. But how can he seem to have asked as if doubting or wanting in faith, who was speaking in mysteries? He was not then doubtful, but careful that we should not doubt. For how could he be doubtful whose prayer was effectual? And how could he have begun the battle without fear, unless he had understood the message of God? for the dew on the fleece signified the faith among the Jews, because the words of God come down like the dew.

7. So when the whole world was parched with the drought of Gentile superstition, then came that dew of the heavenly visits on the fleece. But after that the lost sheep of the house of Israel [794] (whom I think that the figure of the Jewish fleece shadowed forth), after that those sheep, I say, [795] "had refused the fountain of living water," the dew of moistening faith dried up in the breasts of the Jews, and that divine Fountain turned away its course to the hearts of the Gentiles. Whence it has come to pass that now the whole world is moistened with the dew of faith, but the Jews have lost their prophets and counsellors.

8. Nor is it strange that they should suffer the drought of unbelief, whom the Lord deprived of the fertilising of the shower of prophecy, saying: "I will command My clouds that they rain not upon that vineyard." [796] For there is a health-giving shower of salutary grace, as David also said: "He came down like rain upon a fleece, and like drops that drop upon the earth." [797] The divine Scriptures promised us this rain upon the whole earth, to water the world with the dew of the Divine Spirit at the coming of the Saviour. The Lord, then, has now come, and the rain has come; the Lord has come bringing the heavenly drops with Him, and so now we drink, who before

were thirsty, and with an interior draught drink in that Divine Spirit.

9. Holy Gideon, then, foresaw this, that the nations of the Gentiles also would drink by the reception of faith, and therefore he enquired more diligently, for the caution of the saints is necessary. Insomuch that also Joshua the son of Nun, when he saw the captain of the heavenly host, enquired: "Art thou for us, or for our adversaries?" [798] lest, perchance, he might be deceived by some stratagem of the adversary.

10. Nor was it without a reason that he put the fleece neither in a field nor in a meadow, but in a threshing-floor, where is the harvest of the wheat: "For the harvest is plenteous, but the labourers are few;" [799] because that, through faith in the Lord, there was about to be a harvest fruitful in virtues.

11. Nor, again, was it without a reason that he dried the fleece of the Jews, and put the dew from it into a basin, so that it was filled with water, yet he did not himself wash his feet in that dew. The prerogative of so great a mystery was to be given to another. He was being waited for Who alone could wash away the filth of all. Gideon was not great enough to claim this mystery for himself, but "the Son of Man came not to be ministered unto, but to minister." [800] Let us, then, recognize in Whom these mysteries are seen to be accomplished. Not in holy Gideon, for they were still at their commencement. Therefore the Gentiles were surpassed, for dryness was still upon the Gentiles, and therefore did Israel surpass them, for then did the dew remain on the fleece.

12. Let us come now to the Gospel of God. I find the Lord stripping Himself of His garments, and girding Himself with a towel, pouring water into a basin, and washing the disciples'

feet. [801] That heavenly dew was this water, this was foretold, namely, that the Lord Jesus Christ would wash the feet of His disciples in that heavenly dew. And now let the feet of our minds be stretched out. The Lord Jesus wills also to wash our feet, for He says, not to Peter alone, but to each of the faithful: "If I wash not thy feet thou wilt have no part with Me." [802]

13. Come, then, Lord Jesus, put off Thy garments, which Thou didst put on for my sake; be Thou stripped that Thou mayest clothe us with Thy mercy. Gird Thyself for our sakes with a towel, that Thou mayest gird us with Thy gift of immortality. Pour water into the basin, wash not only our feet but also the head, and not only of the body, but also the footsteps of the soul. I wish to put off all the filth of our frailty, so that I also may say: "By night I have put off my coat, how shall I put it on? I have washed my feet, how shall I defile them?" [803]

14. How great is that excellence! As a servant, Thou dost wash the feet of Thy disciples; as God, Thou sendest dew from heaven. Nor dost Thou wash the feet only, but also invitest us to sit down with Thee, and by the example of Thy dignity dost exhort us, saying: "Ye call Me Master and Lord, and ye do well, for so I am. If, then, I the Lord and Master have washed your feet, ye ought also to wash one another's feet." [804]

15. I, then, wish also myself to wash the feet of my brethren, I wish to fulfil the commandment of my Lord, I will not be ashamed in myself, nor disdain what He Himself did first. Good is the mystery of humility, because while washing the pollutions of others I wash away my own. But all were not able to exhaust this mystery. Abraham was, indeed, willing to wash feet, [805] but because of a feeling of hospitality. Gideon, too, was willing to wash the feet of the Angel of the Lord who

appeared to him, [806] but his willingness was confined to one; he was willing as one who would do a service, not as one who would confer fellowship with himself. This is a great mystery which no one knew. Lastly, the Lord said to Peter: "What I do thou knowest not now, but shalt know hereafter." [807] This, I say, is a divine mystery which even they who wash will enquire into. It is not, then, the simple water of the heavenly mystery whereby we attain to be found worthy of having part with Christ.

16. There is also a certain water which we put into the basin of our soul, water from the fleece and from the Book of Judges; water, too, from the Book of Psalms. [808] It is the water of the message from heaven. Let, then, this water, O Lord Jesus, come into my soul, into my flesh, that through the moisture of this rain [809] the valleys of our minds and the fields of our hearts may grow green. May the drops from Thee come upon me, shedding forth grace and immortality. Wash the steps of my mind that I may not sin again. Wash the heel [810] of my soul, that I may be able to efface the curse, that I feel not the serpent's bite [811] on the foot of my soul, but, as Thou Thyself hast bidden those who follow Thee, may tread on serpents and scorpions [812] with uninjured foot. Thou hast redeemed the world, redeem the soul of a single sinner.

17. This is the special excellence of Thy loving-kindness, wherewith Thou hast redeemed the whole world one by one. Elijah was sent to one widow; [813] Elisha cleansed one; [814] Thou, O Lord Jesus, hast at this day cleansed a thousand. How many in the city of Rome, how many at Alexandria, how many at Antioch, how many also at Constantinople! For even Constantinople has received the word of God, and has received evident proofs of Thy judgment. For so long as she cherished

the Arians' poison in her bosom, disquieted by neighbouring wars, she echoed with hostile arms around. But so soon as she rejected those who were alien from the faith she received as a suppliant the enemy himself, the judge of kings, whom she had always been wont to fear, she buried him when dead, and retains him entombed. [815] How many, then, hast Thou cleansed at Constantinople, how many, lastly, at this day in the whole world!

18. Damasus cleansed not, Peter cleansed not, Ambrose cleansed not, Gregory cleansed not; [816] for ours is the ministry, but the sacraments are Thine. For it is not in man's power to confer what is divine, but it is, O Lord, Thy gift and that of the Father, as Thou hast spoken by the prophets, saying: "I will pour out of My Spirit upon all flesh, and their sons and their daughters shall prophesy." [817] This is that typical dew from heaven, this is that gracious rain, as we read: "A gracious rain, dividing for His inheritance." [818] For the Holy Spirit is not subject to any foreign power or law, but is the Arbiter of His own freedom, dividing all things according to the decision of His own will, to each, as we read, severally as He wills. [819]

[783] Judg. vi. 11.

[784] Judg. vi. 14.

[785] Judg. vi. 19-21.

[786] 1 Cor. x. 4.

[787] Num. xi. 4.

[788] Judg. vi. 21.

[789] S. Luke xii. 49.

[790] Judg. vi. 26.

[791] Isa. xi. 2.

[792] S. John viii. 56.

[793] Judg. vi. 36.

[794] S. Matt. xv. 24.

[795] Jer. ii. 13.

[796] Isa. v. 6.

[797] Ps. lxxii. [lxxi.] 6.

[798] Josh. v. 13.

[799] S. Luke x. 2.

[800] S. Matt. xx. 28.

[801] S. John xiii. 4.

[802] S. John xiii. 8.

[803] Cant. v. 3.

[804] S. John xiii. 13, 14.

[805] Gen. xviii. 4.

[806] Whence this statement is derived cannot be ascertained. Possibly it is merely an assumption of St. Ambrose founded on his estimate of Gideon's character.

[807] S. John xiii. 7.

[808] Ps. xxiii. [xxii.] 2.

[809] Ps. lxxv. [lxxiv.] 11.

[810] "Alia est iniquitas nostra, alia calcanei nostri, in quo Adam dente serpentis est vulneratus et obnoxiam hereditatem successionis humanae suo vulnere dereliquit, ut omnes illo vulnere claudicemus." St. Aug. Exp. Psal. xlviii. 6, and St. Ambrose, Enar. in Ps. xlviii. 9: "Unde reor uniquitatem calcanei magis lubricum deliquendi quam reatum aliquem nostri esse delicti." This lubricum delinquendi, the wound of Adam's heel, seems to have been understood of concupiscence, which has the nature of sin, and is called sin by St. Paul.

[811] Gen. iii. 15.

[812] S. Luke x. 19.

[813] 1 [3] Kings xvii. 9.

[814] 2 [4] Kings v. 14.

[815] Athanaricus, king or judex of the West Goths in Dacia, defeated in 369 by the Emperor Valens. Subsequently, in 380, being defeated by the Huns and some Gothic chiefs, he was forced to take refuge in Constantinople, when he was received with all the honour due to his rank. He died the next year.

[816] Damasus of Rome, Peter of Alexandria, Gregory of Constantinople, and St. Ambrose himself. Peter had died by this time, but the fact was probably not yet known at Milan.

[817] Joel ii. 28.

[818] Ps. lxviii. [lxvii.] 9.

[819] 1 Cor. xii. 11.

Chapter I.

St. Ambrose commences his argument by complimenting the Emperor, both for his faith and for the restitution of the Basilica to the Church; then having urged that his opponents, if they affirm that the Holy Spirit is not a servant, cannot deny Him to be above all, adds that the same Spirit, when He said, "All things serve Thee," showed plainly that He was distinct from creatures; which point he also establishes by other evidence.

19. The Holy Spirit, then, is not amongst but above all things. For (since you, most merciful Emperor, are so fully instructed concerning the Son of God as to be able yourself to teach others) I will not detain you longer, as you desire and claim to be told something more exactly [concerning Him], especially since you lately showed yourself to be so pleased by an argument of this nature, as to command the Basilica to be restored to the Church without any one urging you.

20. So, then, we have received the grace of your faith and the reward of our own; for we cannot say otherwise than that it was of the grace of the Holy Spirit, that when all were unconscious of it, you suddenly restored the Basilica. This is the gift, I say, this the work of the Holy Spirit, Who indeed was at that time preached by us, but was working in you.

21. And I do not regret the losses of the previous time, since the sequestration of that Basilica resulted in the gain of a sort of usury. For you sequestrated the Basilica, that you might give proof of your faith. And so your piety fulfilled its intention, which had sequestered that it might give proof, and so gave proof as to restore. I did not lose the fruit, and I have your judgment, and it has been made clear to all that, with a certain

diversity of action, there was in you no diversity of opinion. It was made clear, I say, to all, that it was not of yourself that you sequestrated, that it was of yourself when you restored it.

22. Now let us establish by evidence what we have said. The first point in the discussion is that all things serve. Now it is clear that all things serve, since it is written: "All things serve Thee." [820] This the Spirit said through the prophet. He did not say, We serve, but, "serve Thee," that you might believe that He Himself is excepted from serving. So, then, since all things serve, and the Spirit does not serve, the Holy Spirit is certainly not included amongst all things.

23. For if we say that the Holy Spirit is included amongst all things, certainly when we read that the Spirit searches the deep things of God, [821] we deny that God the Father is over all. For since the Spirit is of God, and is the Spirit of His mouth, how can we say that the Holy Spirit is included amongst all things, seeing that God, Whose is the Spirit, is over all, possessing certainly fulness of perfection and perfect power.

25. But lest the objectors should think that the Apostle was in error, let them learn whom he followed as his authority for his belief. The Lord said in the Gospel: "When the Paraclete is come, Whom I will send to you from My Father, even the Spirit of Truth which proceedeth from the Father, He shall bear witness of Me." [822] So the Holy Spirit both proceeds from the Father, and bears witness of the Son. For the witness Who is both faithful and true bears witness of the Father, than which witness nothing is more full for the expression of the Divine Majesty, nothing more clear as to the Unity of the Divine Power, since the Spirit has the same knowledge as the

Son, Who is the witness and inseparable sharer of the Father's secrets.

26. He excludes, then, the fellowship and number of creatures from the knowledge of God, but by not excluding the Holy Spirit, He shows that He is not of the fellowship of creatures. So that the passage which is read in the Gospel: "For no man hath seen God at any time, save the Only-begotten Son Who is in the bosom of the Father He hath declared Him," also pertains to the exclusion of the Holy Spirit. For how has He not seen God Who searches even the deep things of God? How has He not seen God Who knows the things which are of God? How has He not seen God Who is of God? So, since it is laid down that no one has seen God at any time, whereas the Holy Spirit has seen Him, clearly the Holy Spirit is excepted. He, then, is above all Who is excluded from all.

[820] Ps. cxix. [cxviii.] 91.

[821] 1 Cor. ii. 10.

[822] S. John xv. 26.

Chapter II.
The words, "All things were made by Him," are not a proof that the Holy Spirit is included amongst all things, since He was not made. For otherwise it could be proved by other passages that the Son, and even the Father Himself, must be numbered amongst all things, which would be similar irreverence.

27. This seems, gracious Emperor, to be a full account of our right feeling, but to the impious it does not seem so. Observe what they are striving after. For the heretics are wont to say

that the Holy Spirit is to be reckoned amongst all things, because it is written of God the Son: "All things were made by Him." [823]

28. How utterly confused is a course of argument which does not hold to the truth, and is involved in an inverted order of statements. For this argument would be of value for the statement that the Holy Spirit is amongst all things, if they proved that He was made. For Scripture says that all things which were made were made by the Son; but since we are not taught that the Holy Spirit was made, He certainly cannot be proved to be amongst all things Who was neither made as all things are, nor created. To me this testimony is of use for establishing each point; firstly, that He is proved to be above all things, because He was not made; and secondly, that because He is above all things, He is seen not to have been made, and is not to be numbered amongst those things which were made.

29. But if any one, because the Evangelist stated that all things were made by the Word, making no exception of the Holy Spirit (although the Spirit of God speaking in John said: "All things were made by Him," and said not we were all things which were made; whilst the Lord Himself distinctly showed that the Spirit of God spoke in the Evangelists, saying, "For it will not be you that speak, but the Spirit of your Father that speaketh in you"), [824] yet if any one, as I said, does not except the Holy Spirit in this place, but numbers Him amongst all, he consequently does not except the Son of God in that passage where the Apostle says: "Yet to us there is one God the Father, of Whom are all things, and we by Him." [825] But that he may know that the Son is not amongst all things, let him read what follows, for when he says: "And one Lord Jesus

Christ, by Whom are all things," [826] he certainly excepts the Son of God from all, who also excepted the Father.

30. But it is equal irreverence to detract from the dignity of the Father, or the Son, or the Holy Spirit. For he believes not in the Father who does not believe in the Son, nor does he believe in the Son of God who does not believe in the Spirit, nor can faith stand without the rule of truth. For he who has begun to deny the oneness of power in the Father and the Son and the Holy Spirit certainly cannot prove his divided faith in points where there is no division. So, then, since complete piety is to believe rightly, so complete impiety is to believe wrongly.

31. Therefore they who think that the Holy Spirit ought to be numbered amongst all things, because they read that all things were made by the Son, must needs also think that the Son is to be numbered amongst all things, because they read: "All things are of God." [827] But, consequently, they also do not separate the Father from all things, who do not separate the Son from all creatures, since, as all things are of the Father, so, too, all things are by the Son. And the Apostle, because of his foresight in the Spirit, used this very expression, lest he should seem to the impious who had heard that the Son had said, "That which My Father hath given Me is greater than all," [828] to have included the Son amongst all.

[823] S. John i. 3.

[824] S. Matt. x. 20.

[825] 1 Cor. viii. 6.

[826] 1 Cor. viii. 6.

[827] 2 Cor. v. 18.

[828] S. John x. 29.

Chapter III.

The statement of the Apostle, that all things are of the Father by the Son, does not separate the Spirit from Their company, since what is referred to one Person is also attributed to each. So those baptized in the Name of Christ are held to be baptized in the Name of the Father and of the Holy Spirit, if, that is, there is belief in the Three Persons, otherwise the baptism will be null. This also applies to baptism in the Name of the Holy Spirit. If because of one passage the Holy Spirit is separated from the Father and the Son, it will necessarily follow from other passages that the Father will be subordinated to the Son. The Son is worshipped by angels, not by the Spirit, for the latter is His witness, not His servant. Where the Son is spoken of as being before all, it is to be understood of creatures. The great dignity of the Holy Spirit is proved by the absence of forgiveness for the sin against Him. How it is that such sin cannot be forgiven, and how the Spirit is one.

32. But perhaps some one may say that there was a reason why the writer said that all things were of the Father, and all things through the Son, [829] but made no mention of the Holy Spirit, and would obtain the foundation of an argument from this. But if he persists in his perverse interpretation, in how many passages will he find the power of the Holy Spirit asserted, in which Scripture has stated nothing concerning either the Father or the Son, but has left it to be understood?

40. Where, then, the grace of the Spirit is asserted, is that of God the Father or of the Only-begotten Son denied? By no

means; for as the Father is in the Son, and the Son in the Father, so, too, "the love of God is shed abroad in our hearts by the Holy Spirit, Who hath been given us." [830] And as he who is blessed in Christ is blessed in the Name of the Father, and of the Son, and of the Holy Spirit, because the Name is one and the Power one; so, too, when any divine operation, whether of the Father, or of the Son, or of the Holy Spirit, is treated of, it is not referred only to the Holy Spirit, but also to the Father and the Son, and not only to the Father, but also to the Son and the Spirit.

41. Then, too, the Ethiopian eunuch of Queen Candace, when baptized in Christ, obtained the fulness of the sacrament. And they who said that they knew not of any Holy Spirit, although they said that they had been baptized with John's baptism, were baptized afterwards, because John baptized for the remission of sins in the Name of the coming Jesus, not in his own. And so they knew not the Spirit, because in the form in which John baptized they had not received baptism in the Name of Christ. For John, though he did not baptize in the Spirit, nevertheless preached Christ and the Spirit. And then, when he was questioned whether he were perchance himself the Christ, he answered: "I baptize you with water, but a stronger than I shall come, Whose shoes I am not worthy to bear, He shall baptize you with the Holy Spirit and with fire." [831] They therefore, because they had been baptized neither in the Name of Christ nor with faith in the Holy Spirit, could not receive the sacrament of baptism.

42. So they were baptized in the Name of Jesus Christ, [832] and baptism was not repeated in their case, but administered differently, for there is but one baptism. But where there is not the complete sacrament of baptism, there is not considered to

43

be a commencement nor any kind of baptism. But baptism is complete if one confess the Father, the Son, and the Holy Spirit. If you deny One you overthrow the whole. And just as if you mention in words One only, either the Father, or the Son, or the Holy Spirit, and in your belief do not deny either the Father, the Son, or the Holy Spirit, the mystery of the faith is complete, so, too, although you name the Father, Son, and Holy Spirit, and lessen the power of either the Father, the Son, or the Holy Spirit, the whole mystery is made empty. And, lastly, they who had said: "We have not heard if there be any Holy Spirit, were baptized afterwards in the Name of the Lord Jesus Christ." [833] And this was an additional abundance of grace, for now through Paul's preaching they knew the Holy Spirit.

43. Nor ought it to seem opposed to this, that although subsequently mention is not made of the Spirit, He is yet believed in, and what had not been mentioned in words is expressed in belief. For when it is said, "In the Name of our Lord Jesus Christ," the mystery is complete through the oneness of the Name, and the Spirit is not separated from the baptism of Christ, since John baptized unto repentance, Christ in the Spirit.

44. Let us now consider whether as we read that the sacrament of baptism in the Name of Christ was complete, so, too, when the Holy Spirit alone is named, anything is wanting to the completeness of the mystery. Let us follow out the argument that he who has named One has signified the Trinity. If you name Christ, you imply both God the Father by Whom the Son was anointed, and the Son Himself Who was anointed, and the Holy Spirit with Whom He was anointed. For it is written: "This Jesus of Nazareth, Whom God anointed with the Holy

Spirit." [834] And if you name the Father, you denote equally His Son and the Spirit of His mouth, if, that is, you apprehend it in your heart. And if you speak of the Spirit, you name also God the Father, from Whom the Spirit proceeds, and the Son, inasmuch as He is also the Spirit of the Son.

45. Wherefore that authority may also be joined to reason Scripture indicates that we can also be rightly baptized in the Spirit, when the Lord says: "But ye shall be baptized in the Holy Spirit." [835] And in another place the Apostle says: "For we were all baptized in the body itself into one Spirit." [836] The work is one, for the mystery is one; the baptism one, for there was one death on behalf of the world; there is, then, a oneness of working, a oneness of setting forth, which cannot be separated.

46. But if in this place the Spirit be separated from the operation of the Father and the Son, because it is said, All things are of God, and all things are through the Son, [837] then, too, when the Apostle says of Christ, "Who is over all, God blessed for ever," [838] He set Christ not only above all creatures, but (which it is impious to say) above the Father also. But God forbid, for the Father is not amongst all things, is not amongst a kind of crowd of His own creatures. The whole creation is below, over all is the Godhead of the Father, the Son, and the Holy Spirit. The former serves, the latter rules; the former is subject, the latter reigns; the former is the work, the latter the author of the work; the former, without exception, worships, the latter is worshipped by all without exception.

47. Lastly, of the Son it is written: "And let all the angels of God worship Him." [839] You do not find, Let the Holy Spirit worship. And farther on: "To which of the angels said He at

any time, Sit thou on My right hand till I make thine enemies the footstool of thy feet? Are they not all," says he, "ministering spirits who are sent to minister?" [840] When he says All, does he include the Holy Spirit? Certainly not, because Angels and the other Powers are destined to serve in ministering and obedience to the Son of God.

48. But in truth the Holy Spirit is not a minister but a witness of the Son, as the Son Himself said of Him: "He shall bear witness of Me." [841] The Spirit, then, is a witness of the Son. He who is a witness knows all things, as God the Father is a witness. For so you read in later passages, for our salvation was confirmed to us by God bearing witness by signs and wonders and by manifold powers and by distributions of the Holy Spirit. [842] He who divides as he will is certainly above all, not amongst all, for to divide is the gift of the worker, not an innate part of the work itself.

49. If the Son is above all, through Whom our salvation received its commencement, so that it might be preached, certainly God the Father also, Who testifies and gives confirmation concerning our salvation by signs and wonders, is excepted from all. In like manner the Spirit, Who bears witness to our salvation by His diversities of gifts, is not to be numbered with the crowd of creatures, but to be reckoned with the Father and the Son; Who, when He divides, is not Himself divided by cutting off Himself, for being indivisible He loses nothing when He gives to all, as also the Son, when the Father receives the kingdom, [843] loses nothing, nor does the Father, when He gives that which is His to the Son, suffer loss. We know, then, by the testimony of the Son that there is no loss in the division of spiritual grace; for He Who breathes where He

wills [844] is everywhere free from loss. Concerning which power we shall speak more fully farther on.

50. In the meanwhile, since our intention is to prove in due order that the Spirit is not to be reckoned amongst all things, let us take the Apostle, whose words they call in question, as an authority for this position. For what "all things" would be, whether visible or invisible, he himself declared when he said: "For in Him were all things created in the heavens and in earth." [845] You see that "all things" is spoken of things in the heavens, and of things in earth, for in the heavens are also invisible things which were made.

51. But that no one should be ignorant of this he added those of whom he was speaking: "Whether thrones or dominions or principalities or powers, all things were created by Him and in Him, and He is before all, and in Him all things consist." [846] Does he, then, include the Holy Spirit here amongst creatures? Or when he says that the Son of God is before all things, is he to be supposed to have said that He is before the Father? Certainly not; for as here he says that all things were created by the Son, and that all things in the heavens consist in Him, so, too, it cannot be doubted that all things in the heavens have their strength in the Holy Spirit, since we read: "By the word of the Lord were the heavens established and all the strength of them by the Spirit of His mouth." [847] He, then, is above all, from Whom is all the strength of things in heaven and things on earth. He, then, Who is above all things certainly does not serve; He Who serves not is free; He Who is free has the prerogative of lordship.

52. If I were to say this at first it would be denied. But in the same manner as they deny the less that the greater may not be

believed, so let us set forth lesser matters first that either they may show their perfidy in lesser matters, or, if they grant the lesser matters, we may infer greater from the lesser.

53. I think, most merciful Emperor, that they are most fully confuted who dare to reckon the Holy Spirit amongst all things. But that they may know that they are pressed not only by the testimony of the apostles, but also by that of our Lord; how can they dare to reckon the Holy Spirit amongst all things, since the Lord Himself said: "He who shall blaspheme against the Son of Man, it shall be forgiven him; but he who shall blaspheme against the Holy Ghost shall never be forgiven, either here or hereafter." [848] How, then, can any one dare to reckon the Holy Spirit amongst creatures? Or who will so blind himself as to think that if he have injured any creature he cannot be forgiven in any wise? For if the Jews because they worshipped the host of heaven were deprived of divine protection, whilst he who worships and confesses the Holy Spirit is accepted of God, but he who confesses Him not is convicted of sacrilege without forgiveness: certainly it follows from this that the Holy Spirit cannot be reckoned amongst all things, but that He is above all things, an offence against Whom is avenged by eternal punishment.

54. But observe carefully why the Lord said: "He who shall blaspheme against the Son of Man it shall be forgiven him, but he who shall blaspheme against the Holy Ghost shall never be forgiven, either here or hereafter." [849] Is an offence against the Son different from one against the Holy Spirit? For as their dignity is one, and common to both, so too is the offence. But if any one, led astray by the visible human body, should think somewhat more remissly than is fitting concerning the Body of Christ (for it ought not to appear of little worth to us, seeing it

48

is the palace of chastity, and the fruit of the Virgin), he incurs guilt, but he is not shut out from pardon, which he may attain to by faith. But if any one should deny the dignity, majesty, and eternal power of the Holy Spirit, and should think that devils are cast out not in the Spirit of God, but in Beelzebub, there can be no attaining of pardon there where is the fulness of sacrilege; for he who has denied the Spirit has denied also the Father and the Son, since the same is the Spirit of God Who is the Spirit of Christ.

[829] 1 Cor. viii. 6.

[830] Rom. v. 5.

[831] S. Matt. iii. 11; S. Luke iv. 16; S. John i. 26, 27.

[832] This passage has given rise to the question whether St. Ambrose taught, as some others certainly did (probably on his authority), that baptism in the Name of Christ alone, without mention of the other Persons, is valid. But it is difficult to believe that St. Ambrose meant more than to refer to the passage in the Acts as implying Christian baptism. He says just below that baptism is not complete unless one confess the Father, Son, and Holy Spirit, which would seem to imply the full formula, and he would hardly dissent from St. Basil, who distinctly asserts [De Sp. Sanct. XII.] that baptism without mention of the Three Persons is invalid; and St. Augustine [De Bapt. lib. vi. c. xxv. 47] says that it is more easy to find heretics who reject baptism altogether, than such as omit the right form. Compare also St. Ambrose on St. Luke vi. 67; De Mysteriis, IV. 20; De Sacramentis, II. 5 and 7, especially the latter when he says: In uno nomine...hoc est in nomine Patris et Filii, et Spiritus Sancti.

[833] Acts xix. 5 ff.

[834] Acts x. 38.

[835] Acts i. 5.

[836] 1 Cor. xii. 13.

[837] 1 Cor. viii. 6.

[838] Rom. ix. 5.

[839] Heb. i. 6.

[840] Heb. i. 14.

[841] S. John xv. 26.

[842] Heb. ii. 3, 4.

[843] 1 Cor. xv. 24.

[844] S. John iii. 8.

[845] Col. i. 16.

[846] Col. i. 16, 17.

[847] Ps. xxxiii. [xxxii.] 6.

[848] S. Matt. xii. 32.

[849] S. Matt. xii. 32.

Chapter IV.
The Holy Spirit is one and the same Who spake in the prophets and apostles, Who is the Spirit of God and of

Christ; Whom, further, Scripture designates the Paraclete, and the Spirit of life and truth.

55. But no one will doubt that the Spirit is one, although very many have doubted whether God be one. For many heretics have said that the God of the Old Testament is one, and the God of the New Testament is another. But as the Father is one Who both spake of old, as we read, to the fathers by the prophets, and to us in the last days by His Son; [850] "and as the Son is one, Who according to the tenour of the Old Testament was offended by Adam, [851] seen by Abraham, [852] worshipped by Jacob; [853] so, too, the Holy Spirit is one, who energized in the prophets, [854] was breathed upon the apostles, [855] and was joined to the Father and the Son in the sacrament of baptism. [856] For David says of Him: "And take not Thy Holy Spirit from me." [857] And in another place he said of Him: "Whither shall I go from Thy Spirit?" [858]

56. That you may know that the Spirit of God is the same as the Holy Spirit, as we read also in the Apostle: "No one speaking in the Spirit of God says Anathema to Jesus and no one can say, Lord Jesus, but in the Holy Spirit," [859] the Apostle calls Him the Spirit of God. He called Him also the Spirit of Christ, as you read: "But ye are not in the flesh but in the Spirit, if so be that the Spirit of God dwelleth in you." [860] And farther on: "But if the Spirit of Him Who raised Jesus from the dead dwelleth in you." [861] The same is, then, the Spirit of God, Who is the Spirit of Christ.

57. The same is also the Spirit of Life, as the Apostle says: "For the law of the Spirit of Life in Christ Jesus hath delivered me from the law of sin and death." [862]

58. Him, then, Whom the Apostle called the Spirit of Life, the Lord in the Gospel named the Paraclete, and the Spirit of Truth, as you find: "And I will ask the Father, and He will give you another Comforter [Paraclete], that He may be with you for ever, even the Spirit of Truth, Whom this world cannot receive; because it seeth Him not, neither knoweth Him." [863] You have, then, the Paraclete Spirit, called also the Spirit of Truth, and the invisible Spirit. How, then, do some think that the Son is visible in His Divine Nature, when the world cannot see even the Spirit?

59. Receive now the saying of the Lord, that the same is the Holy Spirit Who is the Spirit of Truth, for you read in the end of this book: "Receive the Holy Spirit." [864] And Peter teaches that the same is the Holy Spirit Who is the Spirit of the Lord, when he says: "Ananias, why has it seemed good to thee to tempt and to lie to the Holy Spirit?" [865] And immediately after he says again to the wife of Ananias: "Why has it seemed good to you to tempt the Spirit of the Lord?" [866] When he says "to you," he shows that he is speaking of the same Spirit of Whom he had spoken to Ananias. He Himself is, then, the Spirit of the Lord Who is the Holy Spirit.

60. And the Lord Himself made clear that the same Who is the Spirit of the Father is the Holy Spirit, when according to Matthew He said that we ought not to take thought in persecution what we should say: "For it is not ye that speak, but the Spirit of your Father that speaketh in you." [867] Again He says according to St. Luke: "Be not anxious how ye shall answer or speak, for the Holy Spirit of God shall teach you in that hour what ye ought to say." [868] So, although many are called spirits, as it is said: "Who maketh His Angels spirits," yet the Spirit of God is but one.

61. Both apostles and prophets received that one Spirit, as the vessel of election, the Doctor of the Gentiles, says: "For we have all drunk of one Spirit;" [869] Him, as it were, Who cannot be divided, but is poured into souls, and flows into the senses, that He may quench the burning of this world's thirst.

[850] Heb. i. 1, 2.

[851] Gen. iii. 17.

[852] Gen. xviii. 22, 23.

[853] Gen. xxviii. 17.

[854] 2 Pet. i. 21.

[855] S. John xx. 22.

[856] S. Matt. xxviii. 19.

[857] Ps. li. [l.] 11.

[858] Ps. cxxxix. [cxxxviii.] 7.

[859] 1 Cor. xii. 3.

[860] Rom. viii. 9.

[861] Rom. viii. 11.

[862] Rom. viii. 2.

[863] S. John xiv. 16, 17.

[864] S. John xx. 22.

[865] Acts v. 3.

[866] Acts v. 9.

[867] S. Matt. x. 20.

[868] S. Luke xii. 11, 12.

[869] 1 Cor. xii. 13.

Chapter V.
The Holy Spirit, since He sanctifies creatures, is neither a creature nor subject to change. He is always good, since He is given by the Father and the Son; neither is He to be numbered amongst such things as are said to fail. He must be acknowledged as the source of goodness. The Spirit of God's mouth, the amender of evils, and Himself good. Lastly, as He is said in Scripture to be good, and is joined to the Father and the Son in baptism, He cannot possibly be denied to be good. He is not, however, said to progress, but to be made perfect in goodness, which distinguishes Him from all creatures.

62. The Holy Spirit is not, then, of the substance of things corporeal, for He sheds incorporeal grace on corporeal things; nor, again, is He of the substance of invisible creatures, for they receive His sanctification, and through Him are superior to the other works of the universe. Whether you speak of Angels, or Dominions, or Powers, every creature waits for the grace of the Holy Spirit. For as we are children through the Spirit, because "God sent the Spirit of His Son into our hearts crying, Abba, Father; so that thou art now not a servant but a son;" [870] in like manner, also, every creature is waiting for the revelation of the sons of God, whom in truth the grace of the Holy Spirit made sons of God. Therefore, also, every creature itself shall be changed by the revelation of the grace of the Spirit, "and shall

be delivered from the bondage of corruption into the liberty of the glory of the children of God." [871]

63. Every creature, then, is subject to change, not only such as has been changed by some sin or condition of the outward elements, but also such as can be liable to corruption by a fault of nature, though by careful discipline it be not yet so; for, as we have shown in a former treatise, [872] the nature of Angels evidently can be changed. It is certainly fitting to judge that such as is the nature of one, such also is that of others. The nature of the rest, then, is capable of change, but the discipline is better.

64. Every creature, therefore, is capable of change, but the Holy Spirit is good and not capable of change, nor can He be changed by any fault, Who does away the faults of all and pardons their sins. How, then, is He capable of change, Who by sanctifying works in others a change to grace, but is not changed Himself.

65. How is He capable of change Who is always good? For the Holy Spirit, through Whom the things that are good are ministered to us, is never evil. Whence two evangelists in one and the same place, in words in differing from each other, have made the same statement, for you read in Matthew: "If you, being evil, know how to give good gifts to your children; how much more shall your Father, Who is in heaven, give good things to them that ask Him." [873] But according to Luke you will find it thus written: "How much more shall your heavenly Father give the Holy Spirit to them that ask Him?" [874] We observe, then, that the Holy Spirit is good in the Lord's judgment by the testimony of the evangelists, since the one has put good things in the place of the Holy Spirit, the other has

named the Holy Spirit in the place of good things. If, then, the Holy Spirit is that which is good, how is He not good?

66. Nor does it escape our notice that some copies have likewise, according to St. Luke: "How much more shall your heavenly Father give a good gift to them that ask Him." This good gift is the grace of the Spirit, which the Lord Jesus shed forth from heaven, after having been fixed to the gibbet of the cross, returning with the triumphal spoils of death deprived of its power, as you find it written: "Ascending up on high He led captivity captive, and gave good gifts to men." [875] And well does he say "gifts," for as the Son was given, of Whom it is written: "Unto us a Child is born, unto us a Son is given;" [876] so, too, is the grace of the Spirit given. But why should I hesitate to say that the Holy Spirit also is given to us, since it is written: "The love of God is shed forth in our hearts by the Holy Spirit, Who is given to us." [877] And since captive breasts certainly could not receive Him, the Lord Jesus first led captivity captive, that our affections being set free, He might pour forth the gift of divine grace.

67. And He said well "led captivity captive." For the victory of Christ is the victory of liberty, which won grace for all, and inflicted wrong on none. So in the setting free of all no one is captive. And because in the time of the Lord's passion wrong alone had no part, which had made captive all of whom it had gained possession, captivity itself turning back upon itself was made captive, not now attached to Belial but to Christ, to serve Whom is liberty. "For he who is called in the Lord as a servant is the Lord's freedman." [878]

68. But to return to the point. "All," says He, "have gone aside, all together are become unprofitable. There is none that doeth

good, not even one." [879] If they except the Holy Spirit, even they themselves confess that He is not amongst all; if they do not except Him, then they, too, acknowledge that He has gone aside amongst all.

69. But let us consider whether He has goodness in Himself, since He is the Source and Principle of goodness. For as the Father and the Son have, so too the Holy Spirit also has goodness. And the Apostle also taught this when he said: "Now the fruit of the Spirit is peace, love, joy, patience, goodness." [880] For who doubts that He is good Whose fruit is goodness. For "a good tree brings forth good fruit." [881]

70. And so if God be good, how shall He Who is the Spirit of His mouth not be good, Who searcheth even the deep things of God? Can the infection of evil enter into the deep things of God? And from this it is seen how foolish they are who deny that the Son of God is good, when they cannot deny that the Spirit of Christ is good, of Whom the Son of God says: "Therefore said I that He shall receive of Mine." [882]

71. Or is the Spirit not good, Who of the worst makes good men, does away sin, destroys evil, shuts out crime, pours in good gifts, makes apostles of persecutors, and priests of sinners? "Ye were," it is said, "sometime darkness, but now are ye light in the Lord." [883]

72. But why do we put them off? And if they ask for statements since they do not deny facts, let them hear that the Holy Spirit is good, for David said: "Let Thy good Spirit lead me forth in the right way." [884] For what is the Spirit but full of goodness? Who though because of His nature He cannot be attained to, yet because of His goodness can be received by us, filling all things His power, but only partaken of by the just, simple in

substance, rich in virtues, present to each, dividing of His own to every one, and Himself whole everywhere.

73. And with good cause did the Son of God say: "Go and baptize all nations in the Name of the Father, and of the Son, and of the Holy Spirit," [885] not disdaining association with the Holy Spirit. Why, then, do some take it ill that He Whom the Lord disdained not in the sacrament of baptism, should be joined in our devotion with the Father and the Son?

74. Good, then, is the Spirit, but good, not as though acquiring but as imparting goodness. For the Holy Spirit does not receive from creatures but is received; as also He is not sanctified but sanctifies; for the creature is sanctified, but the Holy Spirit sanctifies. In which matter, though the word is used in common, there is a difference in the nature. For both the man who receives and God Who gives sanctity are called holy, as we read: "Be ye holy, for I am holy." [886] Now sanctification and corruption cannot share the same nature, and therefore the grace of the Holy Spirit and the creature cannot be of one substance.

75. Since, then, the whole invisible creation (whose substance some rightly believe to be reasonable and incorporeal), with the exception of the Trinity, does not impart but acquires the grace of the Spirit, and does not share in it but receives it, the whole commonalty of creation is to be separated from association with the Holy Spirit. Let them then believe that the Holy Spirit is not a creature; or, if they think Him a creature, why do they associate Him with the Father? If they think Him a creature, why do they join Him with the Son of God? But if they do not think that He should be separated from the Father and the Son,

they do not consider Him to be a creature, for where the sanctification is one the nature is one.

[870] Gal. iv. 6, 7.

[871] Rom. viii. 19, 21.

[872] De Fid. III. 3.

[873] S. Matt. vii. 11.

[874] S. Luke xi. 13.

[875] Ps. lxviii. [lxvii.] 18.

[876] Isa. ix. 6.

[877] Rom. v. 5.

[878] 1 Cor. vii. 22.

[879] Ps. xiv. [xiii.] 3.

[880] Gal. v. 22.

[881] S. Matt. vii. 17.

[882] S. John xvi. 15.

[883] Eph. v. 8.

[884] Ps. cxliii. [cxlii.] 10.

[885] S. Matt. xxviii. 19.

[886] Lev. xix. 2.

Chapter VI.
Although we are baptized with water and the Spirit, the

latter is much superior to the former, and is not therefore to be separated from the Father and the Son.

76. There are, however, many who, because we are baptized with water and the Spirit, think that there is no difference in the offices of water and the Spirit, and therefore think that they do not differ in nature. Nor do they observe that we are buried in the element of water that we may rise again renewed by the Spirit. For in the water is the representation of death, in the Spirit is the pledge of life, that the body of sin may die through the water, which encloses the body as it were in a kind of tomb, that we, by the power of the Spirit, may be renewed from the death of sin, being born again in God.

77. And so these three witnesses are one, as John said: "The water, the blood, and the Spirit." [887] One in the mystery, not in nature. The water, then, is a witness of burial, the blood is a witness of death, the Spirit is a witness of life. If, then, there be any grace in the water, it is not from the nature of water, but from the presence of the Holy Spirit.

78. Do we live in the water or in the Spirit? Are we sealed in the water or in the Spirit. For in Him we live and He Himself is the earnest of our inheritance, as the Apostle says, writing to the Ephesians: "In Whom believing ye were sealed with the Holy Spirit of promise, Who is an earnest of our inheritance." [888] So we were sealed by the Holy Spirit, not by nature, but by God, for it is written: "He Who anointed us is God, Who also sealed us, and gave the earnest of the Spirit in our hearts."

79. We were then sealed with the Spirit by God. For as we die in Christ, in order to be born again, so, too, we are sealed with the Spirit, that we may possess His brightness and image and grace, which is undoubtedly our spiritual seal. For although we

were visibly sealed in our bodies, we are in truth sealed in our hearts, that the Holy Spirit may portray in us the likeness of the heavenly image.

80. Who, then, can dare to say that the Holy Spirit is separated from the Father and the Son, since through Him we attain to the image and likeness of God, and through Him, as the Apostle Peter says, are partakers of the divine nature? In which there is certainly not the inheritance of carnal succession, but the spiritual connection of the grace of adoption. And in order that we may know that this seal is rather on our hearts than on our bodies, the prophet says: "The light of Thy countenance has been impressed upon us, O Lord, Thou hast put gladness in my heart." [889]

[887] 1 John v. 8.

[888] Eph. i. 13, 14.

[889] Ps. iv. 6, 7.

Chapter VII.
The Holy Spirit is not a creature, seeing that He is infinite, and was shed upon the apostles dispersed through all countries, and moreover sanctifies the Angels also, to whom He makes us equal. Mary was full of the same likewise, so too, Christ the Lord, and so far all things high and low. And all benediction has its origin from His operation, as was signified in the moving of the water at Bethesda.

81. Since then, every creature is confined within certain limits of its own nature, and inasmuch as those invisible operations, which cannot be circumscribed by place and bounds, yet are

closed in by the property of their own substance; how can any one dare to call the Holy Spirit a creature, Who has not a limited and circumscribed power? because He is always in all things and everywhere, which assuredly is the property of Divinity and Lordship, for: "The earth is the Lord's and the fulness thereof." [890]

81. And so, when the Lord appointed His servants the apostles, that we might recognize that the creature was one thing and the grace of the Spirit another, He appointed them to different places, because all could not be everywhere at once. But He gave the Holy Spirit to all, to shed upon the apostles though separated the gift of indivisible grace. The persons, then, were different, but the accomplishment of the working was in all one, because the Holy Spirit is one of Whom it is said: "Ye shall receive power, even the Holy Spirit coming upon you, and ye shall be witnesses to Me in Jerusalem and in all Judea and Samaria, and unto the ends of the earth." [891]

82. The Holy Spirit, then, is uncircumscribed and infinite, Who infused Himself into the minds of the disciples throughout the separate divisions of distant regions, and the remote bounds of the whole world, Whom nothing is able to escape or to deceive. And therefore holy David says: "Whither shall I go from Thy Spirit, or whither shall I flee from Thy face." [892] Of what Angel does the Scripture say this? of what Dominion? of what Power? of what Angel do we find the power diffused over many? For Angels were sent to few, but the Holy Spirit was poured upon whole peoples. Who, then, can doubt that that is divine which is shed upon many at once and is not seen; but that that is corporeal which is seen and held by individuals?

83. But in like manner as the Spirit sanctifying the apostles is not a partaker of human nature; so, too, He sanctifying Angels, Dominions, and Powers, has no partnership with creatures. But if any think that the holiness of the Angels is not spiritual, but some other kind of grace belonging to the property of their nature, they will forsooth judge Angels to be inferior to men. For since themselves also confess that they would not dare to compare Angels to the Holy Spirit, and they cannot deny that the Holy Spirit is shed upon men; but the sanctification of the Spirit is a divine gift and favour, men who possess a better kind of sanctification will certainly be found to be preferred to the Angels. But since Angels come down to men to assist them, it must be understood that the nature of Angels is higher as it receives more of the grace of the Spirit, and that the favour awarded to us and to them comes from the same author.

84. But how great is that grace which makes even the lower nature of the lot of men equal to the gifts received by Angels, as the Lord Himself promised, saying: "Ye shall be as the Angels in heaven." Nor is it difficult, for He Who made those Angels in the Spirit will by the same grace make men also equal to the Angels.

85. But of what creature can it be said that it fills all things, as is written of the Holy Spirit: "I will pour My Spirit upon all flesh." [893] This cannot be said of an Angel. Lastly, Gabriel himself, when sent to Mary, said: "Hail, full of grace," [894] plainly declaring the grace of the Spirit which was in her, because the Holy Spirit had come upon her, and she was about to have her womb full of grace with the heavenly Word.

86. For it is of the Lord to fill all things, Who says: "I fill heaven and earth." [895] If, then, it is the Lord Who fills

heaven and earth, Who can judge the Holy Spirit to be without a share in the dominion and divine power, seeing that He has filled the world, and what is beyond the whole world, filled Jesus the Redeemer of the whole world? For it is written: "But Jesus, full of the Holy Spirit, departed from Jordan." [896] Who, then, except one who possessed the same fulness could fill Him Who fills all things?

87. But lest they should object that this was said according to the flesh, though He alone from Whose flesh went forth virtue to heal all, was more than all; yet, as the Lord fills all things, so, too, we read of the Spirit: "For the Spirit of the Lord filled the whole world." [897] And you find it said of all who had consorted with the Apostles that, "filled with the Holy Spirit they spoke the word of God with boldness." [898] You see that the Spirit gives both fulness and boldness, Whose operation the archangel announces to Mary, saying: "The Holy Spirit shall come on thee." [899]

88. You read, too, in the Gospel that the Angel descended at the appointed time into the pool and troubled the water, and he who first went down into the pool was made whole. [900] What did the Angel declare in this type but the descent of the Holy Spirit, which was to come to pass in our day, and should consecrate the waters when invoked by the prayers of the priest? That Angel, then, was a herald of the Holy Spirit, inasmuch as by means of the grace of the Spirit medicine was to be applied to our infirmities of soul and mind. The Spirit, then, has the same ministers as God the Father and Christ. He fills all things, possesses all things, works all and in all in the same manner as God the Father and the Son work.

89. What, then, is more divine than the working of the Holy Spirit, since God Himself testifies that the Holy Spirit presides over His blessings, saying: "I will put My Spirit upon thy seed and My blessings upon thy children." [901] For no blessing can be full except through the inspiration of the Holy Spirit. Wherefore, too, the Apostle found nothing better to wish us than this, as He himself said: "We cease not to pray and make request for you that ye may be filled with the knowledge of His will, in all wisdom and spiritual understanding walking worthily of God." [902] He taught, then, that this was the will of God, that rather by walking in good works and words and affections, we should be filled with the will of God, Who puts His Holy Spirit in our hearts. Therefore if he who has the Holy Spirit is filled with the will of God, there is certainly no difference of will between the Father and the Son.

[890] Ps. xxiv. [xxiii.] 1.

[891] Acts i. 8.

[892] Ps. cxxxix. [cxxviii.] 7.

[893] Joel ii. 28.

[894] S. Luke i. 28.

[895] Jer. xxiii. 24.

[896] S. Luke iv. 1.

[897] Wisd. i. 7.

[898] Acts iv. 31.

[899] S. Luke i. 35.

[900] S. John v. 4.

[901] Isa. xliv. 3.

[902] Col. i. 9.

Chapter VIII.

The Holy Spirit is given by God alone, yet not wholly to each person, since there is no one besides Christ capable of receiving Him wholly. Charity is shed abroad by the Holy Spirit, Who, prefigured by the mystical ointment, is shown to have nothing common with creatures; and He, inasmuch as He is said to proceed from the mouth of God, must not be classed with creatures, nor with things divisible, seeing He is eternal.

90. Observe at the same time that God gives the Holy Spirit. For this is no work of man, nor gift of man; but He Who is invoked by the priest is given by God, wherein is the gift of God and the ministry of the priest. For if the Apostle Paul judged that he was not able to give the Holy Spirit himself by his own authority, and considered himself so far unequal to this office that he wished us to be filled by God with the Spirit, [903] who is sufficient to dare to arrogate to himself the conferring of this gift? So the Apostle uttered this wish in prayer, and did not claim a right by any authority of his own; he desired to obtain, he did not presume to command. Peter, too, says that he is not capable of compelling or restraining the Holy Spirit. For he spoke thus: "Wherefore if God has granted them the same grace as to us, who was I that I could resist God?" [904]

91. But perchance they would not be moved by the example of apostles, and so let us use divine utterances; for it is written:

"Jacob is My servant, I will uphold him; Israel is My elect, My soul hath upheld him, I put My Spirit upon him." [905] The Lord also said by Isaiah: "The Spirit of the Lord is upon Me, because He hath anointed Me." [906]

92. Who, then, can dare to say that the substance of the Holy Spirit is created, at Whose shining in our hearts we behold the beauty of divine truth, and the distance between the creature and the Godhead, that the work may be distinguished from its Author? Or of what creature has God so spoken as to say: "I will pour out of My Spirit"? [907] He said not Spirit, but "of My Spirit," for we are not able to receive the fulness of the Holy Spirit, but we receive as much as our Master divides to us of His own according to His will. [908] For as the Son of God thought it not robbery that He should be equal to God, but emptied Himself, that we might be able to receive Him in our minds; but He emptied Himself not that He was void of His own fulness, but in order that He, Whose fulness I could not endure, might infuse Himself into me according to the measure of my capacity, in like manner also the Father says that He pours out of the Spirit upon all flesh; for He did not pour Him forth wholly, but that which He poured forth abounded for all.

93. There was therefore a pouring out upon us of the Spirit, but upon the Lord Jesus, when He was in the form of man, the Spirit abode, as it is written: "Upon Whom thou shalt see the Spirit descending from heaven, and abiding upon Him, He it is Who baptizeth in the Holy Spirit." [909] Around us is the liberality of the Giver in abundant provision, in Him abides for ever the fulness of the Spirit. He shed forth then what He deemed to be sufficient for us, and what was shed forth is not separated nor divided; but He has a unity of fulness wherewith He may enlighten the sight of our hearts according to what our

strength is capable of. Lastly, we receive so much as the advancing of our mind acquires, for the fulness of the grace of the Spirit is indivisible, but is shared in by us according to the capacity of our own nature.

94. God, then, sheds forth of the Spirit, and the love of God is also shed abroad through the Spirit; in which point we ought to recognize the unity of the operation and of the grace. For as God shed forth of the Holy Spirit, so also "the love of God is shed abroad in our hearts through the Holy Spirit;" [910] in order that we may understand that the Holy Spirit is not a work, Who is the dispenser and plenteous Fount of the divine love.

95. In like manner that you may believe that that which is shed abroad cannot be common to the creatures but peculiar to the Godhead, the name of the Son is also poured forth, as you read: "Thy Name is as ointment poured forth." [911] Of which saying nothing can surpass the force. For as ointment closed up in a vase keeps in its perfume, so long as it is confined in the narrow space of that vase, though it cannot reach many, it yet preserves its strength. But when the ointment has been poured out of that vase wherein it was enclosed, it spreads far and wide; so, too, the Name of Christ before His coming amongst the people of Israel was enclosed in the minds of the Jews as in some vase. For "God is known in Judah, His Name is great in Israel;" [912] that is, the Name which the vases of the Jews held confined in their narrow limits.

96. Even then that Name was indeed great, when it remained in the narrow limits of the weak and few, but it had not yet poured forth its greatness throughout the hearts of the Gentiles, and to the ends of the whole world. But after that He

by His coming had shone throughout the whole world, He spread abroad that divine Name of His throughout all creatures, not filled up by any addition (for fulness admits not of increase), but filling up the empty spaces, that His Name might be wonderful in all the world. The pouring forth, then, of His Name signifies a kind of abundant exuberance of graces and copiousness of heavenly goods, for whatever is poured forth flows over from abundance.

97. So as wisdom which proceeds from the mouth of God cannot be said to be created, nor the Word Which is uttered from His heart, nor the power in which is the fulness of the eternal Majesty; so, too, the Spirit which is poured forth from the mouth of God cannot be considered to be created, since God Himself has shown their unity to be such that He speaks of His pouring forth of His Spirit. By which we understand that the grace of God the Father is the same as that of the Holy Spirit, and that without any division or loss it is divided to the hearts of each. That, then, which is shed abroad of the Holy Spirit is neither severed, nor comprehended in any corporeal parts, nor divided.

98. For how can it be credible that the Spirit should be divided by any parcelling out? John says of God: "Hereby know we that He abides in us by the Spirit which He hath given us." [913] But that which abides always is certainly not changed, therefore if it suffers no change it is eternal. And so the Holy Spirit is eternal, but the creature is liable to fault, and therefore subject to change. But that which is subject to change cannot be eternal, and there cannot therefore be anything in common between the Spirit and the creature, because the Spirit is eternal, but every creature is temporal.

99. But the Apostle also shows that the Holy Spirit is eternal, for: "If the blood of bulls and of goats, and the sprinkling the ashes of an heifer sanctifieth to the purifying of the flesh, how much more the blood of Christ, Who through the eternal Spirit offered Himself without spot to God?" [914] Therefore the Spirit is eternal.

[903] Eph. v. 18.

[904] Acts xi. 17.

[905] Isa. xlii. 1.

[906] Isa. lxi. 1.

[907] Joel ii. 28.

[908] Phil. ii. 6.

[909] S. John i. 33.

[910] Rom. v. 5.

[911] Cant. i. 3.

[912] Ps. lxxvi. [lxxv.] 1.

[913] 1 John iii. 24.

[914] Heb. ix. 13, 14.

Chapter IX.
The Holy Spirit is rightly called the ointment of Christ, and the oil of gladness; and why Christ Himself is not the ointment, since He was anointed with the Holy Spirit. It is not strange that the Spirit should be called Ointment, since the Father and the Son are also called Spirit. And

there is no confusion between them, since Christ alone suffered death, Whose saving cross is then spoken of.

100. Now many have thought that the Holy Spirit is the ointment of Christ. And well it is said ointment, because He is called the oil of gladness, the joining together of many graces giving a sweet fragrance. But God the Almighty Father anointed Him the Prince of priests, Who was, not like others anointed in a type under the Law, but was both according to the Law anointed in the body, and in truth was full with the virtue of the Holy Spirit from the Father above the Law.

101. This is the oil of gladness, of which the prophet says: "God, even Thy God, hath anointed Thee with the oil of gladness above Thy fellows." [915] Lastly, Peter says that Jesus was anointed with the Spirit, as you read: "Ye know that word which went through all Judea beginning from Galilee after the baptism which John preached, even Jesus of Nazareth, how God anointed Him with the Holy Spirit." [916] The Holy Spirit is, then, the oil of gladness.

102. And well did he say oil of gladness, lest you should think Him a creature; for it is the nature of this sort of oil that it will by no means mingle with moisture of another kind. Gladness, too, does not anoint the body, but brightens the inmost heart, as the prophet said: "Thou hast put gladness in my heart." [917] So as he loses his pains who wishes to mix oil with moister matter, because since the nature of oil is lighter than others, when the others settle, it rises and is separated. How do those wretched pedlars think that the oil of gladness can by their tricks be mingled with other creatures, since of a truth corporeal things cannot be mingled with in corporeal, nor things created with uncreated?

102. And well is that called oil of gladness wherewith Christ was anointed; for neither was usual nor common oil to be sought for Him, wherewith either wounds are dressed or heat assuaged; since the salvation of the world did not seek alleviation for His wounds, nor the eternal might of His wearied Body demand refreshment.

103. Nor is it wonderful if He have the oil of gladness, Who made those about to die rejoice, put off sadness from the world, destroyed the odour of sorrowful death. And so the Apostle says: "For we are the good odour of Christ to God;" [918] certainly showing that he is speaking of spiritual things. But when the Son of God Himself says: "The Spirit of the Lord is upon Me, because He hath anointed Me," [919] He points out the ointment of the Spirit. Therefore the Spirit is the ointment of Christ.

104. Or since the Name of Jesus is as ointment poured out, if they wish to understand Christ Himself, and not the Spirit of Christ to be expressed under the name of ointment, certainly when the Apostle Peter says that the Lord Jesus was anointed with the Holy Spirit, it is without doubt plain that the Spirit also is called ointment.

105. But what wonder, since both the Father and the Son are said to be Spirit. Of which we shall speak more fully when we begin to speak of the Unity of the Name. Yet since most suitable place occurs here, that we may not seem to have passed on without a conclusion, let them read that both the Father is called Spirit, as the Lord said in the Gospel, "for God is Spirit;" [920] and Christ is called Spirit, for Jeremiah said: "The Spirit before our face, Christ the Lord." [921]

106. So, then, both the Father is Spirit and Christ is Spirit, for that which is not a created body is spirit, but the Holy Spirit is not commingled with the Father and the Son, but is distinct from the Father and from the Son. For the Holy Spirit did not die, Who could not die because He had not taken flesh upon Him, and the eternal Godhead was incapable of dying, but Christ died according to the flesh.

107. For of a truth He died in that which He took of the Virgin, not in that which He had of the Father, for Christ died in that nature in which He was crucified. But the Holy Spirit could not be crucified, Who had not flesh and bones, but the Son of God was crucified, Who took flesh and bones, that on that cross the temptations of our flesh might die. For He took on Him that which He was not that He might hide that which He was; He hid that which He was that He might be tempted in it, and that which He was not might be redeemed, in order that He might call us by means of that which He was not to that which He was.

108. O the divine mystery of that cross, on which weakness hangs, might is free, vices are nailed, and triumphal trophies raised. So that a certain saint said: "Pierce my flesh with nails for fear of Thee;" [922] he says not with nails of iron, but of fear and faith. For the bonds of virtue are stronger than those of punishment. Lastly, his faith bound Peter, when he had followed the Lord as far as the hall of the high priest, whom no one had bound, and punishment loosened not him, whom faith bound. Again, when he was bound by the Jews, prayer loosed him, punishment did not hold him, because he had not gone back from Christ.

109. Therefore do you also crucify sin, that you may die to sin; he who dies to sin lives to God; do you live to Him Who spared not His own Son, that in His body He might crucify our passions. For Christ died for us, that we might live in His revived Body. Therefore not our life but our guilt died in Him, "Who," it is said, "bare our sins in His own Body on the tree; that being set free from our sins we might live in righteousness, by the wound of Whose stripes we are healed." [923]

110. That wood of the cross is, then, as it were a kind of ship of our salvation, our passage, not a punishment, for there is no other salvation but the passage of eternal salvation. Whilst expecting death I do not feel it; whilst thinking little of punishment I do not suffer; whilst careless of fear I know it not.

111. Who, then, is He by the wound of Whose stripes we are healed but Christ the Lord? of Whom the same Isaiah prophesied His stripes were our healing, [924] of Whom Paul the Apostle wrote in his epistle: "Who knew no sin, but was made sin for us." [925] This, indeed, was divine in Him, that His Flesh did no sin, nor did the creature of the body take in Him sin. For what wonder would it be if the Godhead alone sinned not, seeing It had no incentives to sin? But if God alone is free from sin, certainly every creature by its own nature can be, as we have said, liable to sin.

[915] Ps. xlv. [xliv.] 8.

[916] Acts x. 37, 38.

[917] Ps. iv. 7.

[918] 2 Cor. ii. 15.

[919] S. Luke iv. 18.

[920] S. John iv. 24.

[921] Lam. iv. 20.

[922] Ps. cxix. [cxviii.] 120.

[923] 1 Pet. ii. 24.

[924] Is. liii. 5.

[925] 2 Cor. v. 21.

Chapter X.
That the Spirit forgives sin is common to Him with the Father and the Son, but not with the Angels.

112. Tell me, then, whoever you are who deny the Godhead of the Holy Spirit. The Spirit could not be liable to sin, Who rather forgives sin. Does an Angel forgive? Does an Archangel? Certainly not, but the Father alone, the Son alone, and the Holy Spirit alone. Now no one is unable to avoid that which he has power to forgive.

113. But perhaps some one will say that the Seraph said to Isaiah: "Behold, this hath touched thy lips, and shall take away thine iniquities, and purge away thy sins." [926] Shall take away, he says, and shall purge, not I will take away, but that fire from the altar of God, that is, the grace of the Spirit. For what else can we piously understand to be on the altar of God but the grace of the Spirit? Certainly not the wood of the forests, nor the soot and coals. Or what is so in accordance with piety as to understand according to the mystery that it was revealed by the mouth of Isaiah that all men should be cleansed by the passion

of Christ, Who as a coal according to the flesh burnt up our sins, as you read in Zechariah: "Is not this a brand cast forth from the fire? And that was Joshua clothed in filthy garments." [927]

114. Lastly, that we may know that this mystery of the common redemption was most clearly revealed by the prophets, you have also in this place: "Lo, it hath taken away thy sins;" [928] not that Christ put aside His sins Who did no sin, but that in the flesh of Christ the whole human race should be loosed from their sins.

115. But even if the Seraph had taken away sin, it would have been as one of the ministers of God appointed to this mystery. For thus said Isaiah: "For one of the Seraphim was sent to me." [929]

[926] Is. vi. 7.

[927] Zech. iii. 2, 3.

[928] Ibid. 4.

[929] Is. vi. 6.

Chapter XI.

The Spirit is sent to all, and passes not from place to place, for He is not limited either by time or space. He goes forth from the Son, as the Son from the Father, in Whom He ever abides: and also comes to us when we receive. He comes also after the same manner as the Father Himself, from Whom He can by no means be separated.

116. The Spirit, also, is indeed said to be sent, but the Seraph to one, the Spirit to all. The Seraph is sent to minister, the Spirit works a mystery. The Seraph performs what is commanded, the Spirit divides as He wills. The Seraph passes from place to place, for he does not fill all things, but is himself filled by the Spirit. The Seraph comes down with a certain mode of passage according to his nature, but we cannot think this of the Spirit, of Whom the Son of God says: "When the Paraclete shall come, even the Spirit of Truth, Whom I send unto you, Who proceedeth from the Father." [930]

117. For if the Spirit proceeds from a place and passes to a place, both the Father Himself will be found in a place, and the Son likewise. If He goes forth from a place, Whom the Father or the Son sends, certainly the Spirit passing from a place, and making progress, seems to leave, according to those impious interpretations, both the Father and the Son like some material body.

118. I am saying this with reference to those who say that the Spirit comes down by movement. But neither the Father, Who is above all not only of corporeal nature, but also of the invisible creation, is circumscribed in any place; nor is the Son, Who, as the Worker of all creation, is above every creature,

enclosed by the places or times of His own works; nor is the Spirit of Truth as being the Spirit of God, circumscribed by any corporeal limits, Who since He is incorporeal is far above the whole rational creation through the ineffable fulness of His Godhead, having over all things the power of breathing where He wills, and of inspiring as He wills. [931]

119. The Spirit is not, then, sent as it were from a place, nor does He proceed as from a place, when He proceeds from the Son, as the Son Himself, when He says, "I came forth from the Father, and am come into the world," [932] destroys all fancies, which can be reckoned as from place to place. In like manner, also, when we read that God is within or without, we certainly do not either enclose God within anybody or separate Him from anybody, but weighing these things in a deep and ineffable estimation, we comprehend the hiddenness of the divine nature.

120. Lastly, Wisdom so says that she came forth from the mouth of the Most High, [933] as not to be external to the Father, but with the Father; for "the Word was with God;" [934] and not only with God but also in God; for He says: "I am in the Father and the Father is in Me." [935] But neither when He goes forth from the Father does He retire from a place, nor is He separated as a body from a body; nor when He is in the Father is He as if a body enclosed as it were in a body. The Holy Spirit also, when He proceeds from the Father and the Son, is not separated from the Father nor separated from the Son. For how could He be separated from the Father Who is the Spirit of His mouth? Which is certainly both a proof of His eternity, and expresses the Unity of this Godhead.

121. He exists then, and abides always, Who is the Spirit of His mouth, but He seems to come down when we receive Him, that He may dwell in us, that we may not be alien from His grace. To us He seems to come down, not that He does come down, but that our mind ascends to Him. Of which we would speak more fully did we not remember that in the former treatise [936] there was set forth that the Father said: "Let us go down and confound their language," [937] and that the Son said: "He that loveth Me will keep My saying, and My Father will love him, and We will come to Him and make Our abode with Him." [938]

122. The Spirit, then, so comes as does the Father, for where the Father is there is also the Son, and where the Son is there is the Holy Spirit. The Holy Spirit, therefore, is not to be supposed to come separately. But He comes not from place to place, but from the disposition of the order to the safety of redemption, from the grace of giving life to that of sanctification, to translate us from earth to heaven, from wretchedness to glory, from slavery to a kingdom.

123. The Spirit comes, then, as the Father comes. For the Son said, "I and the Father will come, and will make Our abode with Him." [939] Does the Father come in a bodily fashion? Thus, then, comes the Spirit in Whom, when He comes, is the full presence of the Father and the Son.

124. But who can separate the Spirit from the Father and the Son, since we cannot even name the Father and the Son without the Spirit? "For no one saith Lord Jesus, except in the Holy Spirit?" [940] If, then, we cannot call Jesus Lord except in the Holy Spirit, we certainly cannot proclaim Him without the Spirit. But if the Angels also proclaim Jesus to be Lord, Whom

no one can proclaim except in the Spirit, then in them also the office of the Holy Spirit operates.

125. We have proved, then, that the presence and the grace of the Father, the Son, and the Holy Spirit are one, which is so heavenly and divine that the Son gives thanks therefore to the Father, saying, "I give thanks to Thee, O Father, Lord of heaven and earth, because Thou hast hidden these things from the wise and prudent, and hast revealed them unto babes." [941]

[930] S. John xv. 26.

[931] S. John iii. 8.

[932] Ibid. xvi. 28.

[933] Eccles. xxiv. 5.

[934] S. John i. 1.

[935] Ibid. xiv. 10.

[936] De Fide, V. 7.

[937] Gen. xi. 7.

[938] S. John xiv. 23.

[939] S. John xiv. 23.

[940] 1 Cor. xii. 3.

[941] S. Matt. xi. 25.

Chapter XII.
The peace and grace of the Father, the Son, and the Holy

Spirit are one, so also is Their charity one, which showed itself chiefly in the redemption of man. Their communion with man is also one.

126. Therefore since the calling is one, the grace is also one. Lastly, it is written: "Grace unto you and peace from God our Father, and from the Lord Jesus Christ." [942] You see, then, that we are told that the grace of the Father and the Son is one, and the peace of the Father and the Son is one, but this grace and peace is the fruit of the Spirit, as the Apostle taught us himself, saying: "But the fruit of the Spirit is love, joy, peace, patience." [943] And peace is good and necessary that no one be troubled with doubtful disputations, nor be shaken by the storm of bodily passions, but that his affections may remain quietly disposed as to the worship of God, with simplicity of faith and tranquillity of mind.

127. As to peace we have proved the point; but as to grace the prophet Zechariah says, that God promised to pour upon Jerusalem the spirit of grace and mercy, [944] and the Apostle Peter says: "Repent and be baptized every one of you in the Name of the Lord Jesus Christ for the remission of sins, and ye shall receive the grace of the Holy Spirit." [945] So grace comes also of the Holy Spirit as of the Father and the Son. For how can there be grace without the Spirit, since all divine grace is in the Spirit?

128. Nor do we read only of the peace and grace of the Father, the Son, and the Holy Spirit, but also, faithful Emperor, of the love and communion. For of love it has been said: "The grace of our Lord Jesus Christ, and the love of God." [946] We have heard of the love of the Father. The same love which is the Father's is also the Son's. For He Himself said: "He that loveth

Me shall be loved of My Father, and I will love him." [947] And what is the love of the Son, but that He offered Himself for us, and redeemed us with His own blood. [948] But the same love is in the Father, for it is written: "God so loved the world, that He gave His Only-begotten Son." [949]

129. So, then, the Father gave the Son, and the Son gave Himself. Love is preserved and due affection is not wronged, for affection is not wronged where there is no distress in the giving up. He gave one Who was willing, He gave One Who offered Himself, the Father did not give the Son to punishment but to grace. If you enquire into the merit of the deed, enquire into the description of the affection. The vessel of election shows plainly the unity of this divine love, because both the Father gave the Son and the Son gave Himself. The Father gave, Who "spared not His own Son, but gave Him up for us all." [950] And of the Son he also says: "Who gave Himself for me." [951] "Gave Himself," he says. If it be of grace, what do I find fault with. If it be that He suffered wrong, I owe the more.

130. But learn that in like manner as the Father gave the Son, and the Son gave Himself, so, too, the Holy Spirit gave Him. For it is written: "Then was Jesus led by the Spirit into the wilderness to be tempted by the devil." [952] So, too, the loving Spirit gave the Son of God. For as the love of the Father and the Son is one, so, too, we have shown that this love of God is shed abroad by the Holy Spirit, and is the fruit of the Holy Spirit, because "the fruit of the Spirit is love, joy, peace, patience." [953]

131. And that there is communion between the Father and the Son is plain, for it is written: "And our communion is with the Father and with His Son Jesus Christ." [954] And in another

place: "The communion of the Holy Spirit be with you all." [955] If, then, the peace of the Father, the Son, and the Holy Spirit is one, the grace one, the love one, and the communion one, the working is certainly one, and where the working is one, certainly the power cannot be divided nor the substance separated. For, if so, how could the grace of the same working agree?

[942] Rom. i. 7.

[943] Gal. v. 22.

[944] Zech. xii. 10.

[945] Acts ii. 38.

[946] 2 Cor. xiii. 14.

[947] S. John xiv. 21.

[948] Eph. v. 2.

[949] S. John iii. 16.

[950] Rom. viii. 32.

[951] Gal. ii. 20.

[952] S. Matt. iv. 1.

[953] Gal. v. 22.

[954] 1 John i. 3.

[955] 2 Cor. xiii. 14.

Chapter XIII.

St. Ambrose shows from the Scriptures that the Name of the Three Divine Persons is one, and first the unity of the Name of the Son and of the Holy Spirit, inasmuch as each is called Paraclete and Truth.

132. Who, then, would dare to deny the oneness of Name, when he sees the oneness of the working. But why should I maintain the unity of the Name by arguments, when there is the plain testimony of the Divine Voice that the Name of the Father, the Son, and the Holy Spirit is one? For it is written: "Go, baptize all nations in the Name of the Father, and of the Son, and of the Holy Spirit." [956] He said, "in the Name," not "in the Names." So, then, the Name of the Father is not one, that of the Son another, and that of the Holy Spirit another, for God is one; the Names are not more than one, for there are not two Gods, or three Gods.

132. And that He might reveal that the Godhead is one and the Majesty one, because the Name of the Father, the Son, and the Holy Spirit is one, and the Son did not come in one Name and the Holy Spirit in another, the Lord Himself said: "I am come in My Father's Name, and ye did not receive Me, if another shall come in his own name ye will receive him." [957]

133. And Scripture makes clear that that which is the Father's Name, the same is also that of the Son, for the Lord said in Exodus: "I will go before thee in My Name, and will call by My Name the Lord before thee." [958] So, then, the Lord said that He would call the Lord by His Name. The Lord, then, is the Name of the Father and of the Son.

134. But since the Name of the Father and of the Son is one, learn that the same is the Name of the Holy Spirit also, since

the Holy Spirit came in the Name of the Son, as it is written: "But the Paraclete, even the Holy Spirit, Whom the Father will send in My Name, He shall teach you all things." [959] But He Who came in the Name of the Son came also certainly in the Name of the Father, for the Name of the Father and of the Son is one. Thus it comes to pass that the Name of the Father and of the Son is also that of the Holy Spirit. For there is no other Name given under heaven wherein we must be saved. [960]

155. At the same time He showed that the oneness of the Divine Name must be taught, not the difference, since Christ came in the oneness of the Name, but Antichrist will come in his own name, as it is written: "I am come in My Father's Name, and ye did not receive Me, if another shall come in his own name, ye will receive him." [961]

156. We are, then, clearly taught by these passages that there is no difference of Name in the Father, the Son, and the Holy Spirit; and that that which is the Name of the Father is also the Name of the Son, and likewise that which is the Name of the Son is also that of the Holy Spirit, when the Son also is called Paraclete, as is the Holy Spirit. And therefore does the Lord Jesus say in the Gospel: "I will ask My Father, and He shall give you another Paraclete, to be with you for ever, even the Spirit of Truth." [962] And He said well "another," that you might not suppose that the Son is also the Spirit, for oneness is of the Name, not a Sabellian confusion of the Son and of the Spirit. [963]

157. So, then, the Son is one Paraclete, the Holy Spirit another Paraclete; for John called the Son a Paraclete, as you find: "If any man sin, we have a Paraclete [Advocate] with the Father, Jesus Christ." [964] So in like manner as there is a oneness of

name, so, too, is there a oneness of power, for where the Paraclete Spirit is, there is also the Son.

158. For as the Lord says in this place that the Spirit will be forever with the faithful, so, too, does He elsewhere show that He will Himself be forever with the apostles, saying: "Lo, I am with you always, even to the end of the world." [965] Therefore the Son and the Spirit are one, the Name of the Trinity is one, and the Presence one and indivisible.

159. But as we show that the Son is called the Paraclete, so, too, do we show that the Spirit is called the Truth. Christ is the Truth, the Spirit is the Truth, for you find in John's epistle: "For the Spirit is Truth." [966] Not only, then, is the Spirit called the Spirit of Truth, but also the Truth, as the Son is also declared to be the Truth, Who says: "I am the Way, the Truth, and the Life." [967]

[956] S. Matt. xxviii. 19.

[957] S. John v. 43.

[958] Ex. xxxiii. 19.

[959] S. John xiv. 26.

[960] Acts iv. 12.

[961] S. John v. 43.

[962] S. John xiv. 16.

[963] The Sabellians, anxious to maintain the Unity of God, denied the distinction of Persons, identifying the Father and the Son. See D. Chr. B. III. 568, and Blunt, Dict. of Sects, etc., sub voc.

[964] 1 John ii. 1.

[965] S. Matt. xxviii. 20.

[966] 1 John v. 7.

[967] S. John xiv. 6.

Chapter XIV.
Each Person of the Trinity is said in the sacred writings to be Light. The Spirit is designated Fire by Isaiah, a figure of which Fire was seen in the bush by Moses, in the tongues of fire, and in Gideon's pitchers. And the Godhead of the same Spirit cannot be denied, since His operation is the same as that of the Father and of the Son, and He is also called the light and fire of the Lord's countenance.

160. But why should I argue that as the Father is light, so, too, the Son is light, and the Holy Spirit is light? Which certainly pertains to the power of God. For God is Light, as John said: "For God is Light, and in Him is no darkness." [968]

161. But the Son, too, is Light, because "the Life was the Light of men." [969] And the Evangelist, that he might show that he was speaking of the Son of God, says of John the Baptist: "He was not light, but [was sent] to be a witness of the Light. That was the true Light, which lighteth every man that cometh into this world." [970] So, then, since God is Light, and the Son of God the true Light, without doubt the Son of God is true God.

162. And you find elsewhere that the Son of God is Light: "The people that sat in darkness and in the shadow of death have seen a great light." [971] But, which is still more clear, it is said: "For with Thee is the fount of Life, and in Thy light we shall

see light," [972] which means that with Thee, O God the Father Almighty, Who art the Fount of Life, in Thy Son Who is the Light, we shall see the light of the Holy Spirit. As the Lord Himself shows, saying: "Receive ye the Holy Spirit," [973] and elsewhere: "Virtue went out from Him." [974]

163. But who can doubt that the Father is Light, when we read of His Son that He is the Brightness of eternal Light? For of Whom but of the Father is the Son the Brightness, Who both is always with the Father, and always shines, not with unlike but with the same radiance.

164. And Isaiah shows that the Holy Spirit is not only Light but also Fire, saying: "And the light of Israel shall be for a fire." [975] So the prophets called Him a burning Fire, because in those three points we see more intensely the majesty of the Godhead; since to sanctify is of the Godhead, to illuminate is the property of fire and light, and the Godhead is wont to be pointed out or seen in the appearance of fire: "For our God is a consuming Fire," as Moses said. [976]

165. For he himself saw the fire in the bush, and had heard God when the voice from the flame of fire came to him saying: "I am the God of Abraham, and the God of Isaac, and the God of Jacob." [977] The voice came from the fire, and the voice was in the bush, and the fire did no harm. For the bush was burning but was not consumed, because in that mystery the Lord was showing that He would come to illuminate the thorns of our body, and not to consume those who were in misery, but to alleviate their misery; Who would baptize with the Holy Spirit and with fire, that He might give grace and destroy sin. [978] So in the symbol of fire God keeps His intention.

166. In the Acts of the Apostles, also, when the Holy Spirit had descended upon the faithful, the appearance of fire was seen, for you read thus: "And suddenly there was a sound from heaven, as though the Spirit were borne with great vehemence, and it filled all the house where they were sitting, and there appeared unto them cloven tongues like as of fire." [979]

167. For the same reason was it that when Gideon was about to overcome the Midianites, he commanded three hundred men to take pitchers, and to hold lighted torches inside the pitchers, and trumpets in their right hands. Our predecessors have preserved the explanation received from the apostles, that the pitchers are our bodies, fashioned of clay, which know not fear if they burn with the fervour of the grace of the Spirit, and bear witness to the passion of the Lord Jesus with a loud confession of the Voice.

168. Who, then, can doubt of the Godhead of the Holy Spirit, since where the grace of the Spirit is, there the manifestation of the Godhead appears. By which evidence we infer not a diversity but the unity of the divine power. For how can there be a severance of power, where the effect of the working in all is one?

169. What, then, is that fire? Not certainly one made up of common twigs, or roaring with the burning of the reeds of the woods, but that fire which improves good deeds like gold, and consumes sins like stubble. This is undoubtedly the Holy Spirit, Who is called both the fire and light of the countenance of God; light as we said above: "The light of Thy countenance has been sealed upon us, O Lord." [980] What is, then, the light that is sealed, but that of the seal of the Spirit, believing in

Whom, "ye were sealed," he says, "with the Holy Spirit of promise." [981]

170. And as there is a light of the divine countenance, so, too, does fire shine forth from the countenance of God, for it is written: "A fire shall burn in His sight." [982] For the grace of the day of judgment shines beforehand, that forgiveness may follow to reward the service of the saints. O the great fulness of the Scriptures, which no one can comprehend with human genius! O greatest proof of the Divine Unity! For how many things are pointed out in these two verses!

[968] 1 John i. 5.

[969] S. John i. 8.

[970] S. John i. 9.

[971] Isa. ix. 2.

[972] Ps. xxxvi. [xxxv.] 9.

[973] S. John xx. 22.

[974] S. Luke vi. 19.

[975] Isa. x. 17.

[976] Deut. iv. 24.

[977] Ex. iii. 6.

[978] S. Matt. iii. 11.

[979] Acts ii. 2, 3.

[980] Ps. iv. 6.

[981] Eph. i. 13.

[982] Ps. l. [xlix.] 3.

Chapter XV.
The Holy Spirit is Life equally with the Father and the Son, in truth whether the Father be mentioned, with Whom is the Fount of Life, or the Son, that Fount can be none other than the Holy Spirit.

171. We have said that the Father is Light, the Son is Light, and the Holy Spirit is Light; let us also learn that the Father is Life, the Son Life, and the Holy Spirit Life. For John said: "That which was from the beginning, that which we have heard, and which we have seen, and have beheld with our eyes, and our hands have handled concerning the Word of Life; and the Life appeared, and we saw and testify, and declare to you of that Life which was with the Father." [983] He said both Word of Life and Life that he might signify both the Father and the Son to be Life. For what is the Word of Life but the Word of God? And by this phrase both God and the Word of God are shown to be Life. And as it is said the Word of Life, so, too, the Spirit of Life. Therefore, as the Word of Life is Life, so, too, the Spirit of Life is Life.

172. Learn now that as the Father is the Fount of Life, so, too, many have stated that the Son is signified as the Fount of Life; [984] so that, he says, with Thee, Almighty God, Thy Son is the Fount of Life. That is the Fount of the Holy Spirit, [985] for the Spirit is Life, as the Lord says: "The words which I speak unto you are Spirit and Life," [986] for where the Spirit is, there also is Life; and where Life is, is also the Holy Spirit.

173. Many, however, consider that in this passage the Father only is signified by the Fount. Let them, however, notice what the Scripture relates: "With Thee is the Well of Life." That is, the Son is with the Father; since the Word was with God, Who was in the beginning, and was with God.

174. But whether in this place one understands the Fount to be the Father or the Son, we certainly do not understand a fount of that water which is created, but the Fount of that divine grace, that is, of the Holy Spirit, for He is the living water. Wherefore the Lord said: "If thou knowest the gift of God, and Who He is that saith to thee, Give me to drink, thou wouldst have asked Him, and He would have given thee living water." [987]

175. This was the water for which the soul of David thirsted. The hart desires the fountain of these waters, [988] not thirsting for the poison of serpents. For the water of the grace of the Spirit is living, that it may purify the inner parts of the mind, and wash away every sin of the soul, and purify the transgression of hidden faults.

[983] 1 John i. 1, 2.

[984] Ps. xxxvi. [xxxv.] 9.

[985] In these words St. Ambrose appears plainly to set forth the procession of the Holy Spirit from the Son, though he admits that some consider the Father to be the Fount of Life, but he argues even in this case the Son was with Him.

[986] S. John vi. 64.

[987] S. John iv. 10.

[988] Ps. xlii. [xli.] 3.

Chapter XVI.

The Holy Spirit is that large river by which the mystical Jerusalem is watered. It is equal to its Fount, that is, the Father and the Son, as is signified in holy Scripture. St. Ambrose himself thirsts for that water, and warns us that in order to preserve it within us, we must avoid the devil, lust, and heresy, since our vessels are frail, and that broken cisterns must be forsaken, that after the example of the Samaritan woman and of the patriarchs we may find the water of the Lord.

176. But lest perchance any one should speak against as it were the littleness of the Spirit, and from this should endeavour to establish a difference in greatness, arguing that water seems to be but a small part of a Fount, although examples taken from creatures seem by no means suitable for application to the Godhead; yet lest they should judge anything injuriously from this comparison taken from creatures, let them learn that not only is the Holy Spirit called Water, but also a River, as we read: "From his belly shall flow rivers of living water. But this He said of the Spirit, Whom they were beginning to receive, who were about to believe in Him." [989]

177. So, then, the Holy Spirit is the River, and the abundant River, which according to the Hebrews flowed from Jesus in the lands, as we have received it prophesied by the mouth of Isaiah. [990] This is the great River which flows always and never fails. And not only a river, but also one of copious stream and overflowing greatness, as also David said: "The stream of the river makes glad the city of God." [991]

178. For neither is that city, the heavenly Jerusalem, watered by the channel of any earthly river, but that Holy Spirit, proceeding from the Fount of Life, by a short draught of Whom we are satiated, seems to flow more abundantly among those celestial Thrones, Dominions and Powers, Angels and Archangels, rushing in the full course of the seven virtues of the Spirit. For if a river rising above its banks overflows, how much more does the Spirit, rising above every creature, when He touches the as it were low-lying fields of our minds, make glad that heavenly nature of the creatures with the larger fertility of His sanctification.

179. And let it not trouble you that either here it is said "rivers," [992] or elsewhere "seven Spirits," [993] for by the sanctification of these seven gifts of the Spirit, as Isaiah said, [994] is signified the fulness of all virtue; the Spirit of wisdom and understanding, the Spirit of counsel and strength, the Spirit of knowledge and godliness, and the Spirit of the fear of God. One, then, is the River, but many the channels of the gifts of the Spirit. This River, then, goes forth from the Fount of Life.

180. And here, again, you must not turn aside your thoughts to lower things, because there seems to be some difference between a Fount and a River, and yet the divine Scripture has provided that the weakness of human understanding should not be injured by the lowliness of the language. Set before yourself any river, it springs from its fount, but is of one nature, of one brightness and beauty. And do you assert rightly that the Holy Spirit is of one substance, brightness, and glory with the Son of God and with God the Father. I will sum up all in the oneness of the qualities, and shall not be afraid of any question as to difference of greatness. For in this point also Scripture has provided for us; for the Son of God says: "He that shall drink

of the water which I will give him, it shall become in him a well of water springing up unto everlasting life." [995] This well is clearly the grace of the Spirit, a stream proceeding from the living Fount. The Holy Spirit, then, is also the Fount of eternal life.

181. You observe, then, from His words that the unity of the divine greatness is pointed out, and that Christ cannot be denied to be a Fount even by heretics, since the Spirit, too, is called a Fount. And as the Spirit is called a river, so, too, the Father said: "Behold, I come down upon you like a river of peace, and like a stream overflowing the glory of the Gentiles." [996] And who can doubt that the Son of God is the River of life, from Whom the streams of eternal life flowed forth?

182. Good, then, is this water, even the grace of the Spirit. Who will give this Fount to my breast? Let it spring up in me, let that which gives eternal life flow upon me. Let that Fount overflow upon us, and not flow away. For Wisdom says: "Drink water out of thine own vessels, and from the founts of thine own wells, and let thy waters flow abroad in thy streets." [997] How shall I keep this water that it flow not forth, that it glide not away? How shall I preserve my vessel, lest any crack of sin penetrating it, should let the water of eternal life exude? Teach us, Lord Jesus, teach us as Thou didst teach Thine apostles, saying: "Lay not up for yourselves treasures upon the earth, where rust and moth destroy, and where thieves break through and steal." [998]

182. For He intimates that the thief is the unclean spirit, who cannot find entrance into those who walk in the light of good works, but if he has caught any one in the darkness of earthly desires, and in the midst of the enjoyment of earthly pleasures,

he spoils them of all the flower of eternal virtue. And therefore the Lord says: "Lay up for yourselves treasures in heaven, where neither rust nor moth destroy, and where thieves do not break through and steal. For where thy treasure is, there will thy heart be also."

183. Our rust is wantonness, our rust is lust, our rust is luxury, which dim the keen vision of the mind with the filth of vices. Again, our moth is Arius, our moth is Photinus, who rend the holy vesture of the Church with their impiety, and desiring to separate the indivisible unity of the divine power, gnaw the precious veil of faith with sacrilegious tooth. The water is spilt if Arius has imprinted his tooth, it flows away if Photinus has planted his sting in any one's vessel. We are but of common clay, we quickly feel vices. But no one says to the potter, "Why hast Thou made me thus?" [999] For though our vessel be but common, yet one is in honour, another in dishonour. [1000] Do not then lay open thy pool, dig not with vices and crimes, lest any one say: "He hath opened a pool and digged it, and is fallen into the pit which he made." [1001]

184. If you seek Jesus, forsake the broken cisterns, for Christ was wont to sit not by a pool but by a well. There that Samaritan woman [1002] found Him, she who believed, she who wished to draw water. Although you ought to have come in early morning, nevertheless if you come later, even at the sixth hour, you will find Jesus wearied with His journey. He is weary, but it is through thee, because He has long sought thee, thy unbelief has long wearied Him. Yet He is not offended if thou only comest, He asks to drink Who is about to give. But He drinks not the water of a stream flowing by, but thy salvation; He drinks thy good dispositions, He drinks the cup, that is, the Passion which atoned for thy sins, that thou

drinking of His sacred blood mightest quench the thirst of this world.

185. So Abraham gained God after he had dug the well. [1003] So Isaac, while walking by the well, received that wife [1004] who was coming to him as a type of the Church. Faithful he was at the well, unfaithful at the pool. Lastly, too, Rebecca, as we read, found him who sought her at the well, and the harlots washed themselves in the blood in the pool of Jezebel. [1005]

[989] John vii. 38, 39.

[990] Is. lxvi. 12.

[991] Ps. xlvi. [xlv.] 4.

[992] S. John vii. 38.

[993] Rev. v. 6.

[994] Isa. xi. 2.

[995] S. John iv. 14.

[996] Isa. lxvi. 12.

[997] Prov. v. 15, 16.

[998] S. Matt. vi. 19.

[999] Rom. ix. 20.

[1000] Rom. ix. 21.

[1001] Ps. vii. 15.

[1002] S. John iv. 6.

[1003] Gen. xxi. 30.

[1004] Gen. xxiv. 62.

[1005] 1 [3] Kings xxii. 36.

Book II.

Introduction.

The Three Persons of the Godhead were not unknown to the judges of old nor to Moses, for the equality of the Son with the Father, as well as of the Three Persons amongst Themselves, is laid down both elsewhere and by him. Samson also enjoyed the assistance of the Holy Spirit, his history is touched upon and shown to be in some points typical of the Church and her mysteries. When the Holy Spirit left Samson he fell into various calamities, and St. Ambrose explains the spiritual significance of his shorn locks.

1. Even in reading the first book of the ancient history it is made clear both that the sevenfold grace of the Spirit shone forth in the judges themselves of the Jews, and that the mysteries of the heavenly sacraments were made known by the Spirit, of Whose eternity Moses was not ignorant. Then, too, at the very beginning of the world, and indeed before its beginning, he conjoined Him with God, Whom he knew to be eternal before the beginning of the world. For if any one takes good heed he will recognize in the beginning both the Father, the Son, and the Spirit. For of the Father it is written: "In the beginning God created the heaven and the earth." [1006] Of the Spirit it is said: "The Spirit was borne upon the waters." [1007] And well in the beginning of creation is there set forth the figure of baptism whereby the creature had to be purified. And of the Son we read that He it is Who divided light from darkness, for there is one God the Father Who speaks, and one God the Son Who acts.

2. But, again, that you may not think that there was assumption in the bidding of Him Who spoke, or inferiority on the part of Him Who carried out the bidding, the Father acknowledges the Son as equal to Himself in the execution of the work, saying: "Let Us make man after Our image and likeness." [1008] For the common image and the working and the likeness can signify nothing but the oneness of the same Majesty.

3. But that we may more fully recognize the equality of the Father and the Son, as the Father spoke, the Son made, so, too, the Father works and the Son speaks. The Father works, as it is written: "My Father worketh hitherto." [1009] You find it said to the Son: "Say the word and he shall be healed." [1010] And the Son says to the Father: "I will that where I am, they too shall be with Me." [1011] The Father did what the Son said.

4. But neither was Abraham ignorant of the Holy Spirit; he saw Three and worshipped One, for there is one God, one Lord, and one Spirit. And so there is a oneness of honour, because there is a oneness of power.

5. And why should I speak of all one by one? Samson, born by the divine promise, had the Spirit accompanying him, for we read: "The Lord blessed him, and the Spirit of the Lord began to be with him in the camp." [1012] And so foreshadowing the future mystery, he demanded a wife of the aliens, which, as it is written, his father and mother knew not of, because it was from the Lord. And rightly was he esteemed stronger than others, because the Spirit of the Lord guided him, under Whose guidance he alone put to flight the people of the aliens, and at another time inaccessible to the bite of the lion, he, unconquerable in his strength, tore him asunder with his hands.

Would that he had been as careful to preserve grace, as strong to overcome the beast!

6. And perhaps this was not only a prodigy of valour, but also a mystery of wisdom, an utterance of prophecy. For it does not seem to have been without a purpose that, as he was going to his marriage, a roaring lion met him, which he tore asunder with his hands, in whose body, when about to enjoy the wished-for wedlock, he found a swarm of bees, and took honey from its mouth, which he gave to his father and mother to eat. The people of the Gentiles which believed had honey, the people which was before savage is now the people of Christ.

7. Nor is the riddle without mystery, which he set forth to his companions: "Out of the eater came forth meat, and out of the strong came forth sweetness." [1013] And there was a mystery up to the point of the three days in which its answer was sought in vain, which could not be made known except by the faith of the Church, on the seventh day, the time of the Law being completed, after the Passion of the Lord. For thus you find that the apostles did not understand, "because Jesus was not yet glorified." [1014]

8. "What," answer they, "is sweeter than honey, and what is stronger than a lion?" To which he replied: "If ye had not farmed with my heifer, you would not have found out my riddle." [1015] O divine mystery! O manifest sacrament! we have escaped from the slayer, we have overcome the strong one. The food of life is now there, where before was the hunger of a miserable death. Dangers are changed into safety, bitterness into sweetness. Grace came forth from the offence, power from weakness, and life from death.

9. There are, however, who think on the other hand that the wedlock could not have been established unless the lion of the tribe of Judah had been slain; and so in His body, that is, the Church, bees were found who store up the honey of wisdom, because after the Passion of the Lord the apostles believed more fully. This lion, then, Samson as a Jew slew, but in it he found honey, as in the figure of the heritage which was to be redeemed, that the remnant might be saved according to the election of grace. [1016]

10. "And the Spirit of the Lord," it is said, "came upon him, and he went down to Ascalon, and smote thirty men of them." [1017] For he could not fail to carry off the victory who saw the mysteries. And so in the garments they receive the reward of wisdom, the badge of intercourse, who resolve and answer the riddle.

11. Here, again, other mysteries come up, in that his wife is taken away, and for this foxes set fire to the sheaves of the aliens. For their own cunning often deceives those who contend against divine mysteries. Wherefore it is said again in the Song of Songs: "Take us the little foxes which destroy the vineyards, that our vineyards may flourish." [1018] He said well "little," because the larger could not destroy the vineyards, though to the strong even the devil is weak.

12. So, then, he (to sum up the story briefly, for the consideration of the whole passage is reserved for its own season) was unconquered so long as he kept the grace of the Spirit, as was the people of God chosen by the Lord, that Nazarite under the Law. Samson, then, was unconquered, and so invincible as to be able to smite a thousand men with the jawbone of an ass; [1019] so full of heavenly grace that when

thirsty he found even water in the jawbone of an ass, whether
you consider this as a miracle, or turn it to a mystery, because
in the humility of the people of the Gentiles there would be
both rest and triumph according to that which is written: "He
that smiteth thee on the cheek, turn to him also the other."
[1020] For by this endurance of injuries, which the sacrament
of baptism teaches, we triumph over the stings of anger, that
having passed through death we may attain to the rest of the
resurrection.

13. Is that, then, Samson who broke ropes twisted with thongs,
and new cords like weak threads? Is that Samson who did not
feel the bonds of his hair fastened to the beam, so long as he
had the grace of the Spirit? He, I say, after the Spirit of God
departed from him, was greatly changed from that Samson
Who returned clothed in the spoils of the aliens, but fallen
from his greatness on the knees of a woman, caressed and
deceived, is shorn of his hair. [1021]

14. Was, then, the hair of his head of such importance that, so
long as it remained, his strength should endure unconquered,
but when his head was shorn the man should suddenly lose all
his strength? It is not so, nor may we think that the hair of his
head has such power. There is the hair of religion and faith; the
hair of the Nazarite perfect in the Law, consecrated in
sparingness and abstinence, with which she (a type of the
Church), who poured ointment on the feet of the Lord, wiped
the feet of the heavenly Word, for then she knew Christ also
after the flesh. That hair it is of which it is said: "Thy hair is as
flocks of goats," [1022] growing on that head of which it is said:
"The head of the man is Christ," [1023] and in another place:
"His head is as fine gold, and his locks like black pine-trees."
[1024]

15. And so, also, in the Gospel our Lord, pointing out that some hairs are seen and known, says: "But even the hairs of your head are all numbered," [1025] implying, indeed, acts of spiritual virtues, for God does not take care for our hair. Though, indeed, it is not absurd to believe that literally, seeing that according to His divine Majesty nothing can be hidden from Him.

16. But what does it profit me, if God Himself knows all my hairs? That rather abounds and profits me, if the watchful witness of good works reward me with the gift of eternal life. And, in fine, Samson himself, declaring that these hairs are not mystical, says: "If I be shorn my strength will depart from me." [1026] So much concerning the mystery, let us now consider the order of the passage.

[1006] Gen. i. 1.

[1007] Gen. i. 4.

[1008] Gen. i. 26.

[1009] S. John v. 17.

[1010] S. Matt. viii. 8.

[1011] S. John xvii. 24.

[1012] Judg. xiii. 25.

[1013] Judg. xiv. 14.

[1014] S. John vii. 39.

[1015] Judg. xiv. 18.

[1016] Rom. xi. 5.

[1017] Judg. xiv. 19.

[1018] Cant. ii. 15.

[1019] Judg. xv. 15.

[1020] S. Matt. v. 39.

[1021] Judg. xvi. 7, 11, 19.

[1022] Cant. iv. 1.

[1023] 1 Cor. xi. 3.

[1024] Cant. v. 11.

[1025] S. Matt. x. 30.

[1026] Judg. xvi. 17.

Chapter I.
The Spirit is the Lord and Power; and in this is not inferior to the Father and the Son.

17. Above, you read that "the Lord blessed him, and the Spirit of the Lord began to go with him." [1027] Farther on it is said: "And the Spirit of the Lord came upon him." [1028] Again he says: "If I be shaven, my strength will depart from me." [1029] After he was shaven, see what the Scripture says: "The Lord," he says, "departed from him." [1030]

18. You see, then, that He Who went with him, Himself departed from him. The Same is, then, the Lord, Who is the Spirit of the Lord, that is, he called the Spirit of God, Lord, as also the Apostle says: "The Lord is the Spirit, now where the

Spirit of the Lord is, there is liberty." You find, then, the Holy Spirit called the Lord; for the Holy Spirit and the Son are not one Person [unus] but one Substance [unum].

19. In this place he used the word Power, and implied the Spirit. For as the Father is Power, so, too, the Son is Power, and the Holy Spirit is Power. Of the Son you have read that Christ is "the Power of God and the Wisdom of God." [1031] We read, too, that the Father is Power, as it is written: "Ye shall see the Son of Man sitting at the right hand of the Power of God." [1032] He certainly named the Father Power, at Whose right hand the Son sits, as you read: "The Lord said unto My Lord, Sit Thou on My right hand." [1033] And the Lord Himself named the Holy Spirit Power, when He said: "Ye shall receive Power when the Holy Spirit cometh upon you." [1034]

[1027] Judg. xiii. 25.

[1028] Judg. xiv. 6.

[1029] Judg. xvi. 17.

[1030] Judg. xvi. 20.

[1031] 1 Cor. i. 24.

[1032] S. Matt. xxvi. 64.

[1033] Ps. cx. [cix.] 1.

[1034] Acts i. 8.

Chapter II.
The Father, the Son, and the Holy Spirit are One in counsel.

20. For the Spirit Himself is Power, as you read: "The Spirit of Counsel and of Power (or might)." [1035] And as the Son is the Angel of great counsel, so, too, is the Holy Spirit the Spirit of Counsel, that you may know that the Counsel of the Father, the Son, and the Holy Spirit is One. Counsel, not concerning any doubtful matters, but concerning those foreknown and determined.

21. But that the Spirit is the Arbiter of the Divine Counsel, you may know even from this. For when above [1036] we showed that the Holy Spirit was the Lord of baptism, and read that baptism is the counsel of God, as you read, "But the Pharisees despised the counsel of God, not being baptized of Him," [1037] it is quite clear that as there can be no baptism without the Spirit, so, too, the counsel of God is not without the Spirit.

22. And that we may know more completely that the Spirit is Power, we ought to know that He was promised when the Lord said: "I will pour out of My Spirit upon all flesh." [1038] He, then, Who was promised to us is Himself Power, as in the Gospel the same Son of God declared when He said: "And I will send the promise of the Father upon you, but do you remain in the city until ye be endued with power from on high." [1039]

23. And the Evangelist so far shows that the Spirit is Power, that St. Luke relates that He came down with great power, when he says: "And suddenly there was a sound from heaven, as though the Spirit were borne with great power." [1040]

24. But, again, that you may not suppose that this is to be referred to bodily things and perceptible to the senses, learn that the Spirit so descended as Christ is to descend, as you find: "They shall see the Son of Man coming in the clouds with great power and majesty." [1041]

25. For how should not the power and might be one, when the work is one, the judgment one, the temple one, the life-giving one, the sanctification one, and the kingdom also of the Father, Son, and Holy Spirit one?

[1035] Isa. xi. 2.

[1036] Book I. vi.

[1037] S. Luke vii. 30.

[1038] Joel ii. 28.

[1039] S. Luke xxiv. 49.

[1040] Acts ii. 2.

[1041] S. Matt. xxiv. 30.

Chapter III.
As to know the Father and the Son is life, so is it life to know the Holy Spirit; and therefore in the Godhead He is not to be separated from the Father.

26. Let them say, then, wherein they think that there is an unlikeness in the divine operation. Since as to know the Father and the Son is life, as the Lord Himself declared, saying: "This is life eternal to know Thee the only true God, and Jesus Christ, Whom Thou hast sent," [1042] so, too, to know the Holy Spirit is life. For the Lord said: "If ye love Me, keep My

commandments, and I will ask the Father and He shall give you another Paraclete, that He may abide with you for ever, even the Spirit of Truth, Whom the world cannot receive, because it seeth Him not, neither knoweth Him, but ye know Him, for He is with you, and in you." [1043]

27. So, then, the world had not eternal life, because it had not received the Spirit; for where the Spirit is, there is eternal life; for the Spirit Himself it is Who effects eternal life. Wherefore I wonder why the Arians stir the question as to the only true God. For as it is eternal life to know the only true God, so, too, is it eternal life to know Jesus Christ; so, again, it is eternal life to know the Holy Spirit, Whom, as also the Father, the world does not see, and, as also the Son, does not know. But he who is not of this world has eternal life, and the Spirit, Who is the Light of eternal life, remains with him for ever.

28. If the knowledge of the only true God confers the same benefit as the knowledge of the Son and of the Spirit, why do you sever the Son and the Spirit from the honour of the true God, when you do not sever Him from conferring the benefit? For of necessity you must either believe that this is the greatest gift of the only true Godhead, and will confess the only true Godhead as of the Father, so also of the Son and of the Holy Spirit; or if you say that he, too, can give life eternal who is not true God, it will happen that you derogate rather from the Father, Whose work you do not consider to be the chief work of the only true Godhead, but one to be compared to the work of a creature.

[1042] S. John xvii. 3.

[1043] S. John xvii. 14, 15.

Chapter IV.
The Holy Spirit gives life, not in a different way from the Father and the Son, nor by a different working.

29. And what wonder is it the Spirit works Life, Who quickens as does the Father and as does the Son? And who can deny that quickening is the work of the Eternal Majesty? For it is written: "Quicken Thy servant." [1044] He, then, is quickened who is a servant, that is, man, who before had not life, but received the privilege of having it.

30. Let us then see whether the Spirit is quickened, or Himself quickens. Now it is written: "The letter killeth, but the Spirit giveth life." [1045] So, then, the Spirit quickens.

31. But that you may understand that the quickening of the Father, Son, and Holy Spirit is no separate work, read how there is a oneness of quickening also, since God Himself quickens through the Spirit, for Paul said: "He Who raised up Christ from the dead shall also quicken your mortal bodies because of His Spirit Who dwelleth in you."

[1044] Ps. cxix. [cxviii.] 17.

[1045] Rom. viii. 11.

Chapter V.

The Holy Spirit, as well as the Father and the Son, is pointed out in holy Scripture as Creator, and the same truth was shadowed forth even by heathen writers, but it was shown most plainly in the Mystery of the Incarnation, after touching upon which, the writer maintains his argument from the fact that worship which is due to the Creator alone is paid to the Holy Spirit.

32. But who can doubt that the Holy Spirit gives life to all things; since both He, as the Father and the Son, is the Creator of all things; and the Almighty Father is understood to have done nothing without the Holy Spirit; and since also in the beginning of the creation the Spirit moved upon the water.

33. So when the Spirit was moving upon the water, the creation was without grace; but after this world being created underwent the operation of the Spirit, it gained all the beauty of that grace, wherewith the world is illuminated. And that the grace of the universe cannot abide without the Holy Spirit the prophet declared when he said: "Thou wilt take away Thy Spirit, and they will fail and be turned again into their dust. Send forth Thy Spirit, and they shall be made, and Thou wilt renew all the face of the earth." [1046] Not only, then, did he teach that no creature can stand without the Holy Spirit, but also that the Spirit is the Creator of the whole creation.

34. And who can deny that the creation of the earth is the work of the Holy Spirit, Whose work it is that it is renewed? For if they desire to deny that it was created by the Spirit, since they cannot deny that it must be renewed by the Spirit, they who desire to sever the Persons must maintain that the operation of the Holy Spirit is superior to that of the Father and the Son,

which is far from the truth; for there is no doubt that the restored earth is better than it was created. Or if at first, without the operation of the Holy Spirit, the Father and the Son made the earth, but the operation of the Holy Spirit was joined on afterwards, it will seem that that which was made required His aid, which was then added. But far be it from any one to think this, namely, that the divine work should be believed to have a change in the Creator, an error brought in by Manicheus. [1047]

35. But do we suppose that the substance of the earth exists without the operation of the Holy Spirit, without Whose work not even the expanse of the sky endures? For it is written: "By the Word of the Lord were the heavens established, and all the strength of them by the Spirit of His Mouth." [1048] Observe what he says, that all the strength of the heavens is to be referred to the Spirit. For how should He Who was moving [1049] before the earth was made, be resting when it was being made?

36. Gentile writers, following ours as it were through shadows, because they could not imbibe the truth of the Spirit, have pointed out in their verses that the Spirit within nourishes heaven and earth, and the glittering orbs of moon and stars. [1050] So they deny not that the strength of creatures exists through the Spirit, are we who read this to deny it? But you think that they refer to a Spirit produced of the air. If they declared a Spirit of the air to be the Author of all things, do we doubt that the Spirit of God is the Creator of all things?

37. But why do I delay with matters not to the purpose? Let them accept a plain proof that there can be nothing which the Holy Spirit can be said not to have made; and that it cannot be

doubted that all subsists through His operation, whether Angels, Archangels, Thrones, or Dominions; since the Lord Himself, Whom the Angels serve, was begotten by the Holy Spirit coming upon the Virgin, as, according to Matthew, the Angel said to Joseph: "Joseph, thou son of David, fear not to take Mary thy wife, for that which shall be born of her is of the Holy Spirit." [1051] And according to Luke, he said to Mary: "The Holy Spirit shall come upon thee." [1052]

38. The birth from the Virgin was, then, the work of the Spirit. The fruit of the womb is the work of the Spirit, according to that which is written: "Blessed art thou among women, and blessed is the Fruit of thy womb." [1053] The flower from the root is the work of the Spirit, that flower, I say, of which it was well prophesied: "A rod shall go forth from the root of Jesse, and a flower shall rise from his root." [1054] The root of Jesse the patriarch is the family of the Jews, Mary is the rod, Christ the flower of Mary, Who, about to spread the good odour of faith throughout the whole world, budded forth from a virgin womb, as He Himself said: "I am the flower of the plain, a lily of the valley." [1055]

39. The flower, when cut, keeps its odour, and when bruised increases it, nor if torn off does it lose it; so, too, the Lord Jesus, on the gibbet of the cross, neither failed when bruised, nor fainted when torn; and when He was cut by that piercing of the spear, being made more beautiful by the colour of the outpoured Blood, He, as it were, grew comely again, not able in Himself to die, and breathing forth upon the dead the gift of eternal life. On this flower, then, of the royal rod the Holy Spirit rested.

40. A good rod, as some think, is the Flesh of the Lord, which, raising itself from its earthly root to heaven, bore around the whole world the sweet-smelling fruits of religion, the mysteries of the divine generation, pouring grace on the altars of heaven.

41. So, then, we cannot doubt that the Spirit is Creator, Whom we know as the Author of the Lord's Incarnation. For who can doubt when you find in the commencement of the Gospel that the generation of Jesus Christ was on this wise: "When Mary was espoused to Joseph, before they came together she was found with child of [ex] the Holy Spirit." [1056]

42. For although most authorities read "de Spiritu," yet the Greek from which the Latins translated have "ech pneumatos hagiou," that is, "ex Spiritu Sancto." For that which is "of" [ex] any one is either of his substance or of his power. Of his substance, as the Son, Who says: "I came forth of the Mouth of the Most High;" [1057] as the Spirit, "Who proceedeth from the Father;" [1058] of Whom the Son says: "He shall glorify Me, for He shall receive of Mine." [1059] But of the power, as in the passage: "One God the Father, of Whom are all things." [1060]

43. How, then, was Mary with child of the Holy Spirit? If as of her substance, was the Spirit, then, changed into flesh and bones? Certainly not. But if the Virgin conceived as of His operation and power, who can deny that the Holy Spirit is Creator?

44. How is it, too, that Job plainly set forth the Spirit as his Creator, saying: "The Spirit of God hath made me"? [1061] In one short verse he showed Him to be both Divine and Creator. If, then, the Spirit is Creator, He is certainly not a creature, for

the Apostle has separated the Creator and the creature, saying: "They served the creature rather than the Creator." [1062]

45. He teaches that the Creator is to be served by condemning those who serve the creature, whereas we owe our service to the Creator. And since he knew the Spirit to be the Creator, he teaches that we ought to serve Him, saying: "Beware of the dogs, beware of the evil workers, beware of the concision, for we are the circumcision who serve the Spirit of God." [1063]

46. But if any one disputes because of the variations of the Latin codices, some of which heretics have falsified, let him look at the Greek codices, and observe that it is there written: "hoi pneumati Theou latreuontes," which is, being translated, "who serve the Spirit of God."

47. So, then, when the same Apostle says that we ought to serve the Spirit, who asserts that we must not serve the creature, but the Creator; without doubt he plainly shows that the Holy Spirit is Creator, and is to be venerated with the honour due to the eternal Godhead; for it is written: "Thou shalt worship the Lord thy God, and Him only shalt thou serve." [1064]

[1046] Ps. civ. [ciii.] 29, 30.

[1047] Manes, or Manicheus, born about a.d. 240, seems to have desired to blend Christianity and Zoroastrianism. The fundamental point of his teaching was the recognition of a good and an evil creator. For a full account, see art. "Manicheans," in Dict. Ch. Biog.

[1048] Ps. xxxiii. [xxxii.] 6.

[1049] Gen. i. 1.

[1050] Virg. AEn. VI. 724.

[1051] S. Matt. i. 20.

[1052] S. Luke i. 35.

[1053] S. Luke i. 42.

[1054] Isa. xi. 1.

[1055] Cant. ii. 1.

[1056] S. Matt. i. 18.

[1057] Ecclus. xxiv. 3.

[1058] S. John xv. 20.

[1059] S. John xvi. 14.

[1060] 1 Cor. viii. 6. The argument from the exact force of prepositions is often urged by the Fathers, as by St. Athanasius and St. Basil among the Greeks. The Latins also use it, as St. Ambrose here, but occasionally the same Greek prepositions are variously rendered, which destroys the force of the argument. With regard to the two prepositions ex and de St. Augustine gives a very good explanation, De Natura Bon, c. 27: "Ex ipso [of Him] does not always mean the same as de ipso [from Him]. That which is from Him can be said to be of Him, but not everything which is of Him is rightly said to be from Him. Of Him are the heavens and the earth, for He made them, but not from Him, because not of His substance." But neither the Vulgate nor even St. Ambrose himself is quite consistent in this matter.

[1061] Job xxxiii. 4.

[1062] Rom. i. 25.

[1063] Phil. iii. 2, 3.

[1064] S. Matt. iv. 10.

Chapter VI.

To those who object that according to the words of Amos the Spirit is created, the answer is made that the word is there understood of the wind, which is often created, which cannot be said of the Holy Spirit, since He is eternal, and cannot be dissolved in death, or by an heretical absorption into the Father. But if they pertinaciously contend that this passage was written of the Holy Spirit, St. Ambrose points out that recourse must be had to a spiritual Interpretation, for Christ by His coming established the thunder, that is, the force of the divine utterances, and by Spirit is signified the human soul as also the flesh assumed by Christ. And since this was created by each Person of the Trinity, it is thence argued that the Spirit, Who has before been affirmed to be the Creator of all things, was the Author of the Incarnation of the Lord.

48. Nor does it escape my notice that heretics have been wont to object that the Holy Spirit appears to be a creature, because many of them use as an argument for establishing their impiety that passage of Amos, where he spoke of the blowing of the wind, as the words of the prophet made clear. For you read thus: "Behold, I am He that establish the thunders, and create the wind [spirit], [1065] and declare unto man his Christ, that make light and mist, and ascend upon high places, the Lord God Almighty is His Name." [1066]

49. If they make an argument of this, that he said "spirit" was created, Esdras taught us that spirit is created, saying in the fourth book: "And upon the second day Thou madest the spirit of the firmament," [1067] yet, that we may keep to our point, is it not evident that in what Amos said the order of the passage shows that the prophet was speaking of the creation of this world?

50. He begins as follows: "I am the Lord that establish the thunders and create the wind [spirit]." The order of the words itself teaches us; for if he had wished to speak of the Holy Spirit, he would certainly not have put the thunders in the first place. For thunder is not more ancient than the Holy Spirit; though they be ungodly, they still dare not say that. And then when we see what follows concerning light and mist, is it not plain that what is said is to be understood of the creation of this world? For we know by every-day experience, that when we have storms on this earth, thunders come first, blasts of wind follow on, the sky grows black with mists, and light shines again out of the darkness. For the blasts of wind are also called "spirits," as it is written: "Fire and brimstone and the spirit of storm." [1068]

51. And that you might know that he called this "spirit," he says: "establishing thunders and creating the wind [spirit]." For these are often created, when they take place. But the Holy Spirit is eternal, and if any one dares to call Him a creature, still he cannot say that He is daily created like the blast of the wind. Then, again, Wisdom herself, speaking after the mystery of the assumed Body, says: "The Lord created Me." [1069] Although prophesying of things to come, yet, because the coming of the Lord was predestined, it is not said "creates" but "created Me;"

118

that men might believe that the Body of Jesus was begotten of the Virgin Mary, not often, but once only.

52. And so, as to that which the prophet declared as it were of the daily working of God in the thunder and the creation of the wind, it would be impious to understand any such thing of the Holy Spirit, Whom the ungodly themselves cannot deny to exist from before the world. Whence with pious asseveration we testify that He always exists, and abides ever. For neither can He Who before the world was moving upon the waters begin to be visible after the world's creation; or else it would be allowable to suppose that there are many Holy Spirits, Who come into being by as it were a daily production. Far be it from any one to pollute himself with such impiety as to say that the Holy Spirit is frequently or ever created. For I do not understand why He should be frequently created; unless perchance they believe that He dies frequently and so is frequently created. But how can the Spirit of life die? If, then, He cannot die, there is no reason why He should be often created.

53. But they who think otherwise fall into this sacrilege, that they do not distinguish the Holy Spirit; who think that the Word Which was sent forth returns to the Father, and the Spirit Which was sent forth is reabsorbed into God, so that there should be a reabsorption [1070] and a kind of alternation of one changing himself into various forms; whereas the distinction between the Father, Son, and Holy Spirit always abiding and unchangeable, preserves the Unity of its power.

54. But if any one thinks that the word of the prophet is to be explained with reference to the Holy Spirit, because it is said, "declaring unto men His Christ," [1071] he will explain it more

easily of the Lord's Incarnation. For if it troubles you that he said Spirit, and therefore you think that this cannot well be explained of the mystery of the taking of human nature, read on in the Scriptures and you will find that all agrees most excellently with Christ, of Whom it is thoroughly fitting to think that He established the thunders by His coming, that is, the force and sound of the heavenly Scriptures, by the thunder, as it were, of which our minds are struck with astonishment, so that we learn to be afraid, and pay respect to the heavenly oracles.

55. Lastly, in the Gospel the brothers of the Lord were called Sons of Thunder; and when the voice was uttered of the Father, saying, "I have both glorified it and will glorify it again," [1072] the Jews said that it thundered on Him. For although they could not receive the grace of the truth, yet they confessed unwillingly, and in their ignorance were speaking mysteries, so that there resulted a great testimony of the Father to the Son. And in the Book of Job, too, the Scripture says: "And who knows when He will make the power of His thunder?" [1073] Certainly if these words pertained to the thunders of the heavens, he would have said that their force was already made, not about to be made.

56. Therefore he referred the thunders to the words of the Lord, the sound of which went out into all the earth, and we understand the word "spirit" in this place of the soul, which He took endowed with reason and perfect; [1074] for Scripture often designates the soul of man by the word spirit, as you read: "Who creates the spirit of man within him." [1075] So, too, the Lord signified His Soul by the word Spirit, when He said: "Into Thy hands I commend My Spirit." [1076]

120

57. And that you might know that he spoke of the coming down of Jesus, he added that He declared His Christ to men, for in His baptism He declared Him, saying: "Thou art My beloved Son, in Whom I am well pleased." [1077] He declared Him on the mount, saying: "This is My beloved Son, hear ye Him." [1078] He declared Him in His Passion, when the sun hid itself, and sea and earth trembled. He declared Him in the Centurion, who said: "Truly this was the Son of God." [1079]

58. We ought, then, to take this whole passage either to be simply to be understood of that state in which we here live and breathe, or of the mystery of the Lord's Body; for if here it had been stated that the Holy Spirit was created, undoubtedly Scripture would elsewhere have declared the same, as we often read of the Son of God, Who according to the flesh was both made and created.

59. But it is fitting that we should consider His Majesty in the very fact of His taking flesh for us, that we may see His divine power in the very taking of the Body. For as we read that the Father created the mystery of the Lord's Incarnation, the Spirit too created it; and so too we read that Christ Himself created His own Body. For the Father created it, as it is written: "The Lord created Me," [1080] and in another place, "God sent His Son, made of a woman, made under the law." [1081] And the Spirit created the whole mystery, according to that which we read, for "Mary was found with child of the Holy Spirit." [1082]

60. You find, then, that the Father created and the Spirit created; learn, too, that the Son of God also created, when Solomon says: "Wisdom hath made herself a house." [1083] How, then, can the Holy Spirit Who created the mystery of the

Lord's Incarnation, which is above all created things, be Himself a creature?

61. As we have shown above [1084] generally that the Holy Spirit is our Creator according to the flesh in the outer man, let us now show that He is our Creator also according to the mystery of grace. And as the Father creates, so too does the Son create, and so too the Holy Spirit creates, as we read in the words of Paul: "For it is the gift of God, not of works, lest any one should boast. For we are His workmanship created in Christ Jesus in good works." [1085]

[1065] Spiritus is Latin for wind and spirit. See note on S: 63 of this book.

[1066] Amos iv. 13.

[1067] 2 [4] Esdras vi. 41.

[1068] Ps. xi. [x.] 6.

[1069] Prov. viii. 22.

[1070] St. Ambrose would seem to be alluding to a certain party amongst the Sabellians, who, to avoid the charge of being Patripassians, maintained that Christ before His Incarnation was one with the Father, from Whom He then emanated, in Whom after His Passion He was again reabsorbed. Cf. De Fide, V. 162.

[1071] Amos iv. 13.

[1072] S. John xii. 28.

[1073] Job xxvi. 14 [LXX.].

[1074] It has been generally held that our Lord's Soul was from the first endowed with all the fulness of which a human soul is capable, having, for instance, perfect knowledge of all things past, present, and to come: the only limit being that a finite nature cannot possess the infinite attributes of the Godhead.

[1075] Zech. xii. 1.

[1076] S. Luke xxiii. 46.

[1077] S. Matt. iii. 17.

[1078] S. Mark ix. 7.

[1079] S. Mark xv. 39.

[1080] Prov. viii. 12.

[1081] Gal. iv. 4.

[1082] S. Matt. i. 18.

[1083] Prov. ix. 1.

[1084] Ch. V.

[1085] Eph. ii. 8 ff.

Chapter VII.
The Holy Spirit is no less the author of spiritual creation or regeneration than the Father and the Son. The excellence of that creation, and wherein it consists. How we are to understand holy Scripture, when it attributes a body or members to God.

62. So, then, the Father creates in good works, and the Son also, for it is written: "But as many as received Him, to them

gave He power to become the sons of God, even to them who believe on His Name; who were born not of blood, nor of the will of the flesh, nor of the will of man, but of God." [1086]

63. In like manner the Lord Himself also testifies that we are born again of the Spirit according to grace, saying: "That which is born of the flesh is flesh, because it is born of flesh; and that which is born of the Spirit is spirit, because God is Spirit. Marvel not that I said unto you, Ye must be born again. The Spirit breatheth [1087] where He willeth, and thou hearest His voice, but knowest not whence He cometh or whither He goeth, so is every one who is born of the Spirit."

64. It is then clear that the Holy Spirit is also the Author of the grace of the Spirit, since we are created according to God, that we may be made the sons of God. So when He has taken us into His kingdom by the adoption of holy regeneration, do we deny Him that which is His? He has made us heirs of the new birth from above, do we claim the heritage and reject its Author? But the benefit cannot remain when its Author is shut out; the Author is not without the gift, nor the gift without the Author. If you claim the grace, believe the power; if you reject the power, do not ask for the grace. He who has denied the Spirit has at the same time denied the gift. For if the Author be of no account how can His gifts be precious? Why do we grudge the gifts we ourselves receive, diminish our hopes, repudiate our dignity, and deny our Comforter?

65. But we cannot deny Him. Far be it from us to deny that which is so great, since the Apostle says: "But ye brethren, like Isaac, are the children of promise, but as then, he that is born after the flesh persecutes him that is after the Spirit." [1088] Again certainly is understood from what has gone before, is

born after the Spirit. He then who is born after the Spirit is born after God. Now we are born again when we are renewed in our inward affections and lay aside the oldness of the outer man. And so the Apostle says again: "But be ye renewed in the spirit of your mind, and put on the new man which is created according to God in truth and righteousness and holiness." [1089] Let them hear how the Scripture has signified the unity of the divine operation. He who is renewed in the spirit of his mind has put on the new man, which is created according to God.

66. That more excellent regeneration is then the work of the Holy Spirit; and the Spirit is the Author of that new man which is created after the image of God, which no one will doubt to be better than this outer man of ours. Since the Apostle has pointed out that the one is heavenly, the other earthly, when he says: "As is the heavenly, such also are the heavenly." [1090]

67. Since, then, the grace of the Spirit makes that to be heavenly which it can create earthy, we ought to observe by reason though we be without instances. For in a certain place holy Job says: "As the Lord liveth, Who thus judgeth me, and the Almighty, Who hath brought my soul to bitterness (for the Spirit of God which is in my nostrils)." [1091] He certainly did not here signify by His Spirit the vital breath and bodily breathing passages, but signifies the nostrils of the inner man within him, wherewith he gathered in the fragrance of eternal life, and drew in the grace of the heavenly ointment as with a kind of twofold sense.

68. For there are spiritual nostrils, as we read, which the spouse of the Word has, to whom it is said: "And the smell of thy nostrils;" [1092] and in another place: "The Lord smelled a

smell of sweetness." [1093] There are, then, as it were, inward members of a man, whose hands are considered to be in action, his ears in hearing, his feet in a kind of progress in a good work. And so from what is done we gather as it were figures of the members, for it is not suitable for us to imagine anything in the inner man after a fleshly manner.

69. And there are some who suppose that God is fashioned after a bodily manner, when they read of His hand or finger, and they do not observe that these things are written not because of any fashion of a body, since in the Godhead are neither members nor parts, but are expressions of the oneness of the Godhead, that we may believe that it is impossible for either the Son or the Holy Spirit to be separated from God the Father; since the fulness of the Godhead dwells as it were bodily in the substance of the Trinity. For this reason, then, is the Son also called the Right Hand of the Father, as we read: "The Right Hand of the Lord hath done mighty things, the Right Hand of the Lord hath exalted me." [1094]

[1086] S. John i. 12, 13.

[1087] It has been thought well in translating this verse to keep the words "spirit" and "breath" as suiting the argument of St. Ambrose. But there can be little doubt that the ordinary translation is the correct one. Bp. Westcott has the following note: "In Hebrew, Syriac, and Latin the words [for spirit and wind] are identical, and Wiclif and the Rhemish version keep "spirit" in both cases, after the Latin. But at present the retention of one word in both places could only create confusion, since the separation between the material emblem and the power which it was used to describe is complete. The use of the correlative verb (pnei, ch. vi. 18; Rev. vii. 1; Matt. vii.

25, 27; Luke xii. 55; Acts xxvii. 40) and of the word sound (voice) is quite decisive for the literal use of the noun (pneuma), and still at the same time the whole of the phraseology is inspired by the higher meaning. Perhaps also the unusual word (pneuma, 1 Kings xviii. 45; xix. 11; 2 Kings iii. 17) is employed to suggest this. The comparison lies between the obvious physical properties of the wind and the mysterious action of that spiritual influence to which the name "spirit," "wind," was instinctively applied. The laws of both are practically unknown, both are unseen, the presence of both is revealed in their effects."--Westcott on S. John iii. 8.

[1088] Gal. iv. 28, 29.

[1089] Eph. iv. 23, 24.

[1090] 1 Cor. xv. 48.

[1091] Job xxvii. 2, 3.

[1092] Cant. vii. 8.

[1093] Gen. viii. 21.

[1094] Ps. cxviii. [cxvii.] 16.

Chapter VIII.
St. Ambrose examines and refutes the heretical argument that because God is said to be glorified in the Spirit, and not with the Spirit, the Holy Spirit is therefore inferior to the Father. He shows that the particle in can be also used of the Son and even of the Father, and that on the other hand with may be said of creatures without any infringement on the prerogatives of the Godhead; and that

in reality these prepositions simply imply the connection of the Three Divine Persons.

70. But what wonder is it if foolish men question about words, when they do so even about syllables? For some think that a distinction should be made and that God should be praised in the Spirit, but not with the Spirit, and consider that the greatness of the Godhead is to be estimated from one syllable or some custom, arguing that if they consider that God should be glorified in the Spirit, they point to some office of the Holy Spirit, but that if they say that God receives glory or power with the Spirit, they seem to imply some association and communion of the Father, the Son, and the Holy Spirit.

71. But who can separate what is incapable of separation? who can divide that association which Christ shows to be inseparable? "Go," says He, "baptize all nations in the Name of the Father and of the Son and of the Holy Spirit." [1095] Has He changed either a word or a syllable here concerning the Father or the Son or the Holy Spirit? Certainly not. But He says, in the Name of the Father and of the Son and of the Holy Spirit. The expression is the same for the Spirit as for the Father and for Himself. From which is inferred not any office of the Holy Spirit, but rather a sharing of honour or of working when we say "in the Spirit."

72. Consider, too, that this opinion of yours tends to the injury of the Father and the Son, for the latter did not say, "with the Name of the Father and of the Son, and of the Holy Spirit," but in the Name, and yet not any office but the power of the Trinity is expressed in this syllable,

73. Lastly, that you may know that it is not a syllable which prejudices faith, but faith which commends a syllable, Paul also

speaks in Christ. Christ is not less, because Paul spoke in Christ, as you find: "We speak before God in Christ." [1096] As, then, the Apostle says that we speak in Christ, so, too, is that which we speak in the Spirit; as the Apostle himself said: "No man saith Lord Jesus, except in the Holy Spirit." [1097] So, then, in this place not any subjection of the Holy Spirit, but a connection of grace is signified.

74. And that you may know that distinction does not depend upon a syllable, he says also in another place: "And these indeed were you, but ye are washed, but ye are sanctified, but ye are justified in the Name of the Lord Jesus Christ, and in the Spirit of our God." [1098] How many instances of this I can bring forward. For it is written: "Ye are all one in Christ Jesus," [1099] and elsewhere: "To those sanctified in Christ Jesus," [1100] and again: "That we might be the righteousness of God in Him," [1101] and in another place: "Should fall from the chastity which is in Christ Jesus." [1102]

75. But what am I doing? For while I say that like things are written of the Son as of the Spirit, I am rather leading on to this, not that because it is written of the Son, therefore it would appear to be reverently written of the Holy Spirit, but that because the same is written of the Spirit, therefore men allege that the Son's honour is lessened because of the Spirit. For say they, Is it written of God the Father?

76. But let them learn that it is also said of God the Father: "In the Lord I will praise the word;" [1103] and elsewhere: "In God we will do mighty deeds;" [1104] and "My remembrance shall be ever in Thee;" [1105] and "In Thy Name will we rejoice;" [1106] and again in another place: "That his deeds may be manifested, that they are wrought in God;" [1107] and Paul: "In

God Who created all things;" [1108] and again: "Paul and Silvanus and Timotheus to the Church of the Thessalonians in God the Father and the Lord Jesus Christ;" [1109] and in the Gospel: "I in the Father and the Father in Me," and "the Father that dwelleth in Me." [1110] It is also written: "He that glorieth let him glory in the Lord;" [1111] and in another place: "Our life is hid with Christ in God." [1112] Did he here ascribe more to the Son than to the Father in saying that we are with Christ in God? or does our state avail more than the grace of the Spirit, so that we can be with Christ and the Holy Spirit cannot? And when Christ wills to be with us, as He Himself said: "Father, I will that they whom Thou hast given Me be with Me where I am," [1113] would He disdain to be with the Spirit? For it is written: "Ye coming together and my spirit with the power of the Lord Jesus." [1114] Do we then come together in the power of the Lord, and dare to say that the Lord Jesus would not be willing to come together with the Spirit Who does not disdain to come together with us?

77. So the Apostle thinks that it makes no difference which particle you use. For each is a conjunctive particle, and conjunction does not cause separation, for if it divided it would not be called a conjunction.

78. What, then, moves you to say that to God the Father or to His Christ there is glory, life, greatness, or power, in the Holy Spirit, and to refuse to say with the Holy Spirit? Is it that you are afraid of seeming to join the Spirit with the Father and the Son? But hear what is written of the Spirit: "For the law of the Spirit is life in Christ Jesus." [1115] And in another place God the Father says: "They shall worship Thee, and in Thee they shall make supplication." [1116] God the Father says that we ought to pray in Christ; and do you think that it is any

derogation to the Spirit if the glory of Christ is said to be in Him?

79. Hear that what you are afraid to acknowledge of the Spirit, the Apostle did not fear to claim for himself; for he says: "To be dissolved and to be with Christ is much better." [1117] Do you deny that the Spirit, through Whom the Apostle was made worthy of being with Christ, is with Christ?

80. What, then, is the reason that you prefer saying that God or Christ is glorified in the Spirit rather than with the Spirit? Is it because if you say in the Spirit, the Spirit is declared to be less than Christ? Although your making the Lord greater or less is a matter which can be refuted, yet since we read, "For Christ was made sin for us, that we might be the righteousness of God in Him," [1118] He is found chiefest in Whom we are found most low. So, too, elsewhere you read, "For in Him all things consist," [1119] that is, in His power. And the things which consist in Him cannot be compared to Him, because they receive from His power the substance whereby they consist.

81. Do you then understand that God so reigns in the Spirit that the power of the Spirit, as a kind of source of substance, imparts to God the origin of His rule? But this is impious. And so our predecessors [1120] spoke of the unity of power of the Father, the Son, and the Holy Spirit, when they said that the glory of Christ was with the Spirit, that they might declare their inseparable connection.

82. For how is the Holy Spirit separated from the Son, since "the Spirit Himself beareth witness with our spirit that we are sons of God, and if sons, also heirs, heirs, indeed, of God and joint-heirs with Christ." [1121] Who, then, is so foolish as to wish to dissever the eternal conjunction of the Spirit and

131

Christ, when the Spirit by Whom we are made joint-heirs with Christ conjoins even what is severed.

83. "If so be," he says, "we suffer with Him, that we may be also glorified together." [1122] If we then shall be glorified together with Christ through the Spirit, how do we refuse to admit that the Spirit Himself is glorified together with Christ? Do we dissociate the life of Christ and of the Holy Spirit when the Spirit says that we shall live together with the Son of God? For the Apostle says: "If we be dead with Christ we believe that we shall also live with Him;" and then again: "For if we suffer with Him we shall also live with Him, and not only shall we live with Him, but shall be also glorified with Him, and not only be glorified but shall also reign with Him." [1123]

84. No division, then, is implied in those particles, for each is a particle of conjunction. And lastly, we often find in holy Scripture the one inserted and the other understood, as it is written: "I will enter into Thy house in whole burnt-offerings," [1124] that is, "with whole burnt-offerings;" and in another place: "He brought them forth in silver and gold," [1125] that is, "with silver and gold." And elsewhere the Psalmist says: "Wilt Thou not go forth with us in our hosts?" [1126] for that which is really meant, "with our hosts." So, then, in the use of the expression no lessening of honour can be implied, and nothing ought to be deduced derogatory to the honour of the Godhead, it is necessary that with the heart man should believe unto righteousness, and that out of the faith of the heart confession should be made in the mouth unto salvation. But they who believe not with the heart spread what is derogatory with their mouth.

[1095] S. Matt. xxviii. 19.

[1096] 2 Cor. ii. 17.

[1097] 1 Cor. xii. 3.

[1098] 1 Cor. vi. 11.

[1099] Gal. iii. 28.

[1100] 1 Cor. i. 2.

[1101] 2 Cor. v. 21.

[1102] 2 Cor. xi. 3.

[1103] Ps. lvi. [lv.] 4.

[1104] Ps. lx. [lix.] 12.

[1105] Ps. lxxi. [lxx.] 6.

[1106] Ps. lxxxix. [lxxxviii.] 16.

[1107] S. John iii. 21.

[1108] Eph. iii. 9.

[1109] 2 Thess. i. 2.

[1110] S. John xiv. 10.

[1111] 2 Cor. x. 17.

[1112] Col. iii. 3.

[1113] S. John xvii. 24.

[1114] 1 Cor. v. 4.

[1115] Rom. viii. 2.

[1116] Isa. xlv. 14 [LXX.].

[1117] Phil. i. 23.

[1118] 2 Cor. v. 21.

[1119] Col. i. 17.

[1120] See St. Basil, De Sp. Sancto, III. 29.

[1121] Rom. viii. 16, 17.

[1122] Rom. viii. 16, 17.

[1123] 2 Tim. ii. 11, 12.

[1124] Ps. lxvi. [lxv.] 13.

[1125] Ps. cv. [civ.] 37.

[1126] Ps. xliv. [xliii.] 10.

Chapter IX.

A passage of St. Paul abused by heretics, to prove a distinction between the Divine Persons, is explained, and it is proved that the whole passage can be rightly said of each Person, though it refers specially to the Son. It is then proved that each member of the passage is applicable to each Person, and as to say, of Him are all things is applicable to the Father, so may all things are through Him and in Him also be said of Him.

85. Another similar passage is that which they say implies difference, where it is written: "But to us there is one Father, of Whom are all things and we unto Him, and one Lord Jesus Christ, through Whom are all things, and we through Him."

[1127] For they pretend that when it is said "of Him," the matter is signified, when "through Him," either the instrument of the work or some office, but when it is said "in Him," either the place or the time in which all things that are made are seen.

86. So, then, their desire is to prove that there is some difference of substance, being anxious to make a distinction between as it were the instrument, and the proper worker or author, and also between time or place and the instrument. But is the Son, then, alien as regards His Nature from the Father, because an instrument is alien from the worker or author? or is the Son alien from the Spirit, because either time or place is not of the same class as an instrument?

87. Compare now our assertions. They will have it that matter is of God as though of the nature of God, as when you say that a chest is made of wood or a statue of stone; that after this fashion matter has come forth from God, and that the same matter has been made by the Son as if by some sort of instrument; so that they declare that the Son is not so much the Artificer as the instrument of the work; and that all things have been made in the Spirit, as if in some place or time; they attribute each part severally to each Person severally and deny that all are in common.

88. But we show that all things are so of God the Father, that God the Father has suffered no loss because all things are either through Him or in Him, and yet all things are not of Him as if of matter; then, too, that all things are through the Lord the Son, so that He is not deprived of the attribute that all things are of the Son and in Him; and that all things are in the Spirit, so that we may teach that all things are through the Spirit, and all things from the Spirit.

89. For these particles, like those of which we have spoken before, imply each other. For the Apostle did not so say, All things are of God, and all things are through the Son, as to signify that the substance of the Father and the Son could be severed, but that he might teach that by a distinction without confusion the Father is one, the Son another. Those particles, then, are not as it were in opposition to each other, but are as it were allied and agreed, so as often to suit even one Person, as it is written: "For of Him, and through Him, and in Him are all things." [1128]

90. But if you really consider whence the passage is taken you will have no doubt that it is said of the Son. For the Apostle says, according to the prophecy of Isaiah, "Who hath known the mind of the Lord, or who hath been His counsellor?" [1129] And he adds: "For of Him and in Him are all things." Which Isaiah had said of the Artificer of all, as you read: "Who hath measured out the water with his hand, and the heaven with a span, and all the earth with his closed hand? Who hath placed the mountains in scales and the hills in a balance? Who hath known the mind of the Lord, or who hath been His counsellor?" [1130]

91. And the Apostle added: "For of Him, and through Him, and in Him are all things." What is "of Him"? That the nature of everything is of His will, and He is the Author of all things which have come into being. "Through Him" means what? That the establishment and continuance of all things is His gift. What is "in Him"? That all things by a wonderful kind of longing and unspeakable love look upon the Author of their life, and the Giver of their graces and functions, according to that which is written: "The eyes of all look unto Thee," and

"Thou openest Thine hand and fillest every living creature with Thy good pleasure." [1131]

92. And of the Father, too, you may rightly say "of Him," for of Him was the operative Wisdom, Which of His own and the Father's will gave being to all things which were not. "Through Him," because all things were made through His Wisdom. "In Him," because He is the Fount of substantial Life, in Whom we live and move and have our being.

93. Of the Spirit also, as being formed by Him, strengthened by Him, established in Him, we receive the gift of eternal life.

94. Since, then, these expressions seem suitable either to the Father or the Son or the Holy Spirit, it is certain that nothing derogatory is spoken of in them, since we both say that many things are of the Son, and many through the Father, as you find it said of the Son: "That we may be increased through all things in Him, Who is Christ the Head, from Whom," says he, "the whole body, framed and knit together through every joint of the supply for the measure of every part, maketh increase of the body unto the building up of itself in love." [1132] And again, writing to the Colossians of those who have not the knowledge of the Son of God, he says: "Because they hold not the Head, from Whom all the body being supplied and joined together through joints and bands, increaseth to the increase of God." [1133] For we said above that Christ is the Head of the Church. And in another place you read: "Of His fulness have all we received." [1134] And the Lord Himself said: "He shall take of Mine and show it unto you." [1135] And before, He said: "I perceive that virtue is gone out of Me." [1136]

95. In like manner that you may recognize the Unity, it is also said of the Spirit: "For he that soweth in the Spirit shall of the

Spirit reap eternal life." [1137] And John says: "Hereby we know that He is in us because He hath given us of His Spirit." [1138] And the Angel says: "That Which shall be born of her is of the Holy Spirit." [1139] And the Lord says: "That which is born of the Spirit is Spirit." [1140]

96. So, then, as we read that all things are of the Father, so, too, that all things can be said to be of the Son, through Whom are all things; and we are taught by proof that all things are of the Spirit in Whom are all things.

97. Now let us consider whether we can teach that anything is through the Father. But it is written: "Paul the servant of Christ through the will of God;" [1141] and elsewhere: "Wherefore thou art now not a servant but a son, and if a son an heir also through God;" [1142] and again: "As Christ rose from the dead by the glory of God." [1143] And elsewhere God the Father says to the Son: "Behold proselytes shall come to Thee through Me." [1144]

98. You will find many other passages, if you look for things done through the Father. Is, then, the Father less because we read that many things are in the Son and of the Son, and find in the heavenly Scriptures very many things done or given through the Father?

99. But in like manner we also read of many things done through the Spirit, as you find: "But God hath revealed them to us through His Spirit;" [1145] and in another place: "Keep the good deposit through the Holy Spirit;" [1146] and to the Ephesians: "to be strengthened through His Spirit;" [1147] and to the Corinthians: "To another is given through the Spirit the word of wisdom;" [1148] and in another place: "But if through the Spirit ye mortify the deeds of the flesh, ye shall live;" [1149]

and above: "He Who raised Christ from the dead shall also quicken your mortal bodies through the indwelling of His Spirit in you." [1150]

100. But perhaps some one may say, Show me that we can read expressly that all things are of the Son, or that all things are of the Spirit. But I reply, Let them also show that it is written that all things are through the Father. But since we have proved that these expressions suit either the Father or the Son or the Holy Spirit, and that no distinction of the divine power can arise from particles of this kind, there is no doubt but that all things are of Him through Whom all things are; and that all things are through Him through Whom all are; and that we must understand that all things are through Him or of Him in Whom all are. For every creature exists both of the will, and through the operation and in the power of the Trinity, as it is written: "Let Us make man after Our image and likeness;" [1151] and elsewhere: "By the word of the Lord were the heavens established, and all their power by the Spirit of His mouth." [1152]

[1127] 1 Cor. viii. 6.

[1128] Rom. xi. 36.

[1129] Isa. xl. 13.

[1130] Isa. xl. 12.

[1131] Ps. cxlv. [cxliv.] 15, 16.

[1132] Eph. iv. 15, 16.

[1133] Col. ii. 19.

[1134] S. John i. 16.

[1135] S. John xvi. 14.

[1136] S. Luke viii. 46.

[1137] Gal. vi. 8.

[1138] 1 John iv. 13.

[1139] S. Matt. i. 20.

[1140] S. John iii. 6.

[1141] 1 Cor. i. 1.

[1142] Gal. iv. 7.

[1143] Rom. vi. 4.

[1144] Isa. liv. 15 [LXX.].

[1145] 1 Cor. ii. 10.

[1146] 1 Tim. vi. 20.

[1147] Eph. iii. 16.

[1148] 1 Cor. xii. 8.

[1149] Rom. viii. 13.

[1150] Rom. viii. 11.

[1151] Gen. i. 26.

[1152] Ps. xxxiii. 6.

Chapter X.

Being about to prove that the will, the calling, and the commandment of the Trinity is one, St. Ambrose shows that the Spirit called the Church exactly as the Father and the Son did, and proves this by the selection of SS. Paul and Barnabas, and especially by the mission of St. Peter to Cornelius. And by the way he points out how in the Apostle's vision the calling of the Gentiles was shadowed forth, who having been before like wild beasts, now by the operation of the Spirit lay aside that wildness. Then having quoted other passages in support of this view, he shows that in the case of Jeremiah cast into a pit by Jews, and rescued by Abdemelech, is a type of the slighting of the Holy Spirit by the Jews, and of His being honoured by the Gentiles.

101. And not only is the operation of the Father, Son, and Holy Spirit everywhere one but also there is one and the same will, calling, and giving of commands, which one may see in the great and saving mystery of the Church. For as the Father called the Gentiles to the Church, saying: "I will call her My people which was not My people, and her beloved who was not beloved;" [1153] and elsewhere: "My house shall be called a house of prayer for all nations," [1154] so, too, the Lord Jesus said that Paul was chosen by Him to call forth and gather together the Church, as you find it said by the Lord Jesus to Ananias: "Go, for he is a chosen vessel unto Me to bear My name before all nations." [1155]

102. As, then, God the Father called the Church, so, too, Christ called it, and so, too, the Spirit called it, saying: "Separate Me Paul and Barnabas for the work to which I have called them." "So," it is added, "having fasted and prayed, they laid hands on

them and sent them forth. And they, being sent forth by the Holy Spirit, went down to Seleucia." [1156] So Paul received the apostleship by the will not only of Christ, but also of the Holy Spirit, and hastened to gather together the Gentiles.

103. And not only Paul, but also, as we read in the Acts of the Apostles, Peter. For when he had seen in his prayer heaven opened and a certain vessel tied at the four corners, as it were a sheet in which were all kinds of four-footed beasts and wild beasts and fowls of the air, "a voice came to him saying, Arise, Peter, kill and eat. And Peter said, Be it far from me, Lord, I have never eaten anything common or unclean. And again a voice came to him, saying, What God hath cleansed call not thou common. And this was done three times, and the vessel was received back into heaven." [1157] And so when Peter was silently thinking over this with himself, and the servants of Cornelius appointed by the Angel had come to him, the Spirit said to him, "Lo, men are seeking thee, rise therefore, and go down and go with them; doubt not, for I have sent thee." [1158]

104. How clearly did the Holy Spirit express His own power! First of all in that He inspired him who was praying, and was present to him who was entreating; then when Peter, being called, answered, "Lord," and so was found worthy of a second message, because he acknowledged the Lord. But the Scripture declares Who that Lord was, for He Whom he had answered spoke to him when he answered. And the following words show the Spirit clearly revealed, for He Who formed the mystery made known the mystery.

105. Notice, also, that the appearance of the mystery three times repeated expressed the operation of the Trinity. And so

in the mysteries [1159] the threefold question is put, and the threefold answer made, and no one can be cleansed but by a threefold confession. For which reason, also, Peter in the Gospel is asked three times whether he loves the Lord, that by the threefold answer the bonds of the guilt he had contracted by denying the Lord might be loosed.

106. Then, again, because the Angel is sent to Cornelius, the Holy Spirit speaks to Peter: "For the eyes of the Lord are over the faithful of the earth." [1160] Nor is it without a purpose that when He had said before, "What God hath cleansed call not thou common," [1161] the Holy Spirit came upon the Gentiles to purify them, when it is manifest that the operation of the Spirit is a divine operation. But Peter, when sent by the Spirit, did not wait for the command of God the Father, but acknowledged that that message was from the Spirit Himself, and the grace that of the Spirit Himself, when he said: "If, then, God has granted them the same grace as to us, who was I that I should resist God?"

107. It is, then, the Holy Spirit Who has delivered us from that Gentile impurity. For in those kinds of four-footed creatures and wild beasts and birds there was a figure of the condition of man, which appears clothed with the bestial ferocity of wild beasts unless it grows gentle by the sanctification of the Spirit. Excellent, then, is that grace which changes the rage of beasts into the simplicity of the Spirit: "For we also were aforetime foolish, unbelieving, erring, serving divers lusts and pleasures. But now by the renewing of the Spirit we begin to be heirs of Christ, and joint-heirs with the Angels." [1162]

108. Therefore the holy prophet David, seeing in the Spirit that we should from wild beasts become like the dwellers in heaven,

says, "Rebuke the wild beasts of the wood," [1163] evidently signifying, not the wood disturbed by the running of wild beasts, and shaken with the roaring of animals, but that wood of which it is written: "We found it in the fields of the wood." [1164] In which, as the prophet said: "The righteous shall flourish as the palm-tree, and shall be multiplied as the cedar which is in Libanus." [1165] That wood which, shaken in the tops of the trees spoken of in prophecy, shed forth the nourishment of the heavenly Word. That wood into which Paul entered indeed as a ravening wolf, but went forth as a shepherd, for "their sound is gone out into all the earth." [1166]

109. We then were wild beasts, and therefore the Lord said: "Beware of false prophets, which come in sheep's clothing, but inwardly are ravening wolves." [1167] But now, through the Holy Spirit, the rage of lions, the spots of leopards, the craft of foxes, the rapacity of wolves, have passed away from our feelings; great, then, is the grace which has changed earth to heaven, that the conversation of us, who once were wandering as wild beasts in the woods, might be in heaven. [1168]

110. And not only in this place, but also elsewhere in the same book, the Apostle Peter declared that the Church was built by the Holy Spirit. For you read that he said: "God, Which knoweth the hearts of men, bare witness, giving them the Holy Spirit, even as also to us; and He made no distinction between us and them, purifying their hearts by faith." [1169] In which is to be considered, that as Christ is the Cornerstone, Who joined together both peoples into one, so, too, the Holy Spirit made no distinction between the hearts of each people, but united them.

111. Do not, then, like a Jew, despise the Son, Whom the prophets foretold; for you would despise also the Holy Spirit, you would despise Isaiah, you would despise Jeremiah, whom he who was chosen of the Lord raised with rags and cords from the pit of that Jewish abode. [1170] For the people of the Jews, despising the word of prophecy, had cast him into the pit. Nor was there found any one of the Jews to draw the prophet out, but one Ethiopian Abdemelech, as the Scripture testifies.

112. In which account is a very beautiful figure, that is to say, that we, sinners of the Gentiles, black beforehand through our transgressions, and aforetime fruitless, raised from the depth the word of prophecy which the Jews had thrust down, as it were, into the mire of their mind and carnality. And therefore it is written: "Ethiopia shall stretch out her hand unto God." [1171] In which is signified the appearance of holy Church, who says in the Song of Songs: "I am black and comely, O daughters of Jerusalem;" [1172] black through sin, comely through grace; black by natural condition, comely through redemption, or certainly, black with the dust of her labours. So she is black while fighting, is comely when she is crowned with the ornaments of victory.

113. And fittingly is the prophet raised by cords, for the faithful writer said: "The lines are fallen unto me in pleasant places." [1173] And fittingly with rags; for the Lord Himself, when those who had been first invited to the marriage made excuse, sent to the partings of the highways, that as many as were found, both bad and good, should be invited to the marriage. With these rags, then, He lifted the word of prophecy from the mire.

[1153] Hos. ii. 23.

[1154] Isa. lvi. 7.

[1155] Acts ix. 15.

[1156] Acts xiii. 2 ff.

[1157] Acts x. 11 ff.

[1158] Acts x. 19, 20.

[1159] The "mysteries" are the sacrament of baptism, and the "three-fold question" those which preceded baptism, viz.: Dost thou believe in God the Father Almighty? Dost thou believe in our Lord Jesus Christ, and in His cross? and Dost thou believe in the Holy Spirit? with the answer, "I believe," to each, as mentioned by the author of De Sacramentis, II. 7 (written probably in the 5th or 6th century).

[1160] Ps. ci. [c.] 6.

[1161] Acts x. 15.

[1162] Tit. iii. 3-7.

[1163] Ps. lxviii. [lxvii.] 30.

[1164] Ps. cxxxii. [cxxxi] 6.

[1165] Ps. xcii. [xci.] 12.

[1166] Ps. xix. [xviii.] 4.

[1167] S. Matt. vii. 15.

[1168] Phil. iii. 20.

[1169] Acts xv. 8, 9.

[1170] Jer. xxxviii. 11.

[1171] Ps. lxviii. [lxvii.] 31.

[1172] Cant. i. 5.

[1173] Ps. xvi. [xv.] 6.

Chapter XI.
We shall follow the example of Abdemelech, if we believe that the Son and Holy Spirit know all things. This knowledge is attributed in Scripture to the Spirit, and also to the Son. The Son is glorified by the Spirit, as also the Spirit by the Son. Also, inasmuch as we read that the Father, the Son, and the Spirit say and reveal the same things, we must acknowledge in Them a oneness of nature and knowledge. Lastly, that the Spirit searcheth the deep things of God is not a mark of ignorance, since the Father and the Son are likewise said to search, and Paul, although chosen by Christ, yet was taught by the Spirit.

114. And you, too, shall be Abdemelech, [1174] that is, chosen by the Lord, if you raise the Word of God from the depth of Gentile ignorance; if you believe that the Son of God is not deceived, that nothing escapes His knowledge, that He is not ignorant of what is going to be. And the Holy Spirit also is not deceived, of Whom the Lord says: "But when He, the Spirit of Truth, shall come, He shall lead you into all truth." [1175] He Who says all passes by nothing, neither the day nor the hour, neither things past nor things to come.

115. And that you may know that He both knows all things, and foretells things to come, and that His knowledge is one with that of the Father and the Son, hear what the Truth of

God says concerning Him: "For He shall not speak from Himself, but what things He shall hear shall He speak, and He shall declare unto you the things that are to come." [1176]

116. Therefore, that you may observe that He knows all things, when the Son said: "But of that day and hour knoweth no one, not even the Angels of heaven," [1177] He excepted the Holy Spirit. But if the Holy Spirit is excepted from ignorance, how is the Son of God not excepted?

117. But you say that He numbered the Son of God also with the Angels. He numbered the Son indeed, but He did not number the Spirit also. Confess, then, either that the Holy Spirit is greater than the Son of God, so as to speak now not only as an Arian, but even as a Photinian, [1178] or acknowledge to what you ought to refer it that He said that the Son knew not. For as man He could [in His human nature] be numbered with creatures Who were created.

118. But if you are willing to learn that the Son of God knows all things, and has foreknowledge of all, see that those very things which you think to be unknown to the Son, the Holy Spirit received from the Son. He received them, however, through Unity of Substance, as the Son received from the Father. "He," says He, "shall glorify Me, for He shall receive of Mine and shall declare it unto you. All things whatsoever the Father hath are Mine, therefore said I, He shall receive of Mine, and shall declare it unto you." [1179] What, then, is more clear than this Unity? What things the Father hath pertain to the Son; what things the Son hath the Holy Spirit also has received.

119. Yet learn that the Son knows the day of judgment. We read in Zechariah: "And the Lord my God shall come, and all the saints with Him. In that day there shall not be light, but

cold and frost, and it shall be one day, and that day is known unto the Lord." [1180] This day, then, was known unto the Lord, Who shall come with His saints, to enlighten us by His second Advent.

120. But let us continue the point which we have commenced concerning the Spirit. For in the passage we have brought forward you find that the Son says of the Spirit: "He shall glorify Me." So, then, the Spirit glorifies the Son, as the Father also glorifies Him, but the Son of God also glorifies the Spirit, as we said above. He, then, is not weak who is the cause of the mutual glory through the Unity of the Eternal Light, nor is He inferior to the Spirit, of Whom this is true that He is glorified by the Spirit.

122. And you too shall be chosen, if you believe that the Spirit spoke that which the Father spoke, and which the Son spoke. Paul, in fine, was therefore chosen because he so believed and so taught, since, as it is written, God "hath revealed to us by His Spirit that which eye hath not seen, nor ear heard, nor hath entered into the heart of man, the things which God hath prepared for them that love Him." [1181] And therefore is He called the Spirit of revelation, as you read: "For God giveth to those who thus prepare themselves the Spirit of wisdom and revelation, that He may be known." [1182]

123. There is, then, a Unity of knowledge, since, as the Father, Who gives the Spirit of revelation, reveals, so also the Son reveals, for it is written: "No one knoweth the Son save the Father, neither doth any one know the Father save the Son, and he to whom the Son shall will to reveal Him." [1183] He said more concerning the Son, not because He has more than the Father, but lest He should be supposed to have less. And not

149

unfittingly is the Father thus revealed by the Son, for the Son knows the Father even as the Father knows the Son.

124. Learn now that the Spirit too knows God the Father, for it is written that, "As no one knoweth the things of a man, save the spirit which is in him, so too the things of God no one knoweth save the Spirit of God." "No one," he says, "knoweth save the Spirit of God." [1184] Is, then, the Son of God excluded? Certainly not, since neither is the Spirit excluded, when it is said: "And none knoweth the Father, save the Son."

125. Therefore the Father, Son, and Holy Spirit are of one nature and of one knowledge. And the Spirit is not to be numbered with all things which were made by the Son, since He knew the Father, Whom (as it is written) who can know save the Son? But the Holy Spirit knows also. What then? When the totality of created things is spoken of, it follows that the Holy Spirit is not included.

126. Now I should like them to answer what it is in man which knows the things of a man. Certainly that must be reasonable which surpasses the other powers of the soul, and by which the highest nature of man is estimated. What, then, is the Spirit, Who knows the deep things of God, and through Whom Almighty God is revealed? Is He inferior in the fulness of the Godhead Who is proved even by this instance to be of one substance with the Father? Or is He ignorant of anything Who knows the counsels of God, and His mysteries which have been hidden [1185] from the beginning? What is there that He knows not Who knows all things that are of God? For "the Spirit searcheth even the deep things of God." [1186]

127. But lest you should think that He searches things unknown, and so searches that He may learn that which He

knows not, it is stated first that God revealed them to us through His Spirit, and at the same time in order that you may learn that the Spirit knows the things which are revealed to us through the Spirit Himself, it is said subsequently: "For who among men knoweth the things of a man, save the spirit of the man which is in him? so, too, the things of God knoweth no one save the Spirit of God." [1187] If, then, the spirit of a man knows the things of a man, and knows them before it searches, can there be anything of God which the Spirit of God knows not? Of Whom the Apostle said not without a purpose, "The things of God knoweth no one, save the Spirit of God;" not that He knows by searching, but knows by nature; not that the knowledge of divine things is an accident in Him, but is His natural knowledge.

128. But if this moves you that He said "searcheth," learn that this is also said of God, inasmuch as He is the searcher of hearts and reins. For Himself said: "I am He that searcheth the heart and reins." [1188] And of the Son of God you have also in the Epistle to the Hebrews: "Who is the Searcher of the mind and thoughts." [1189] Whence it is clear that no inferior searches the inward things of his superior, for to know hidden things is of the divine power alone. The Holy Spirit, then, is a searcher in like manner as the Father, and the Son is a searcher in like manner, by the proper signification of which expression this is implied, that evidently there is nothing which He knows not, Whom nothing escapes.

129. Lastly, he was chosen by Christ, and taught by the Spirit. For as he himself witnesses, having obtained through the Spirit knowledge of the divine secrets, he shows both that the Holy Spirit knows God, and has revealed to us the things which are of God, as the Son also has revealed them. And he adds: "But

we received, not the spirit of this world, but the Spirit which is of God, that we might know the things that are given to us by God, which we also speak, not in persuasive words of man's wisdom, but in manifestation of the Spirit and in the power of God." [1190]

[1174] Ebedmelech means "servant of the king."

[1175] S. John xvi. 13.

[1176] S. John xvi. 13.

[1177] S. Mark xiii. 32.

[1178] There is some little difficulty in ascertaining exactly what were the tenets of Photinus, but it would appear that St. Ambrose considered that he held our Lord to be mere man, and so was worse than the Arians. See Dict. Chr. Biog. art. "Photinus," and Blunt, Dict. of Sects and Heresies, art. "Photinians."

[1179] S. John xvi. 14, 15.

[1180] Zech. xiv. 5, 6, 7 [LXX.].

[1181] 1 Cor. ii. 9, 10.

[1182] Isa. lxiv. 4.

[1183] S. Matt. xi. 27.

[1184] 1 Cor. ii. 11.

[1185] 1 Cor. ii. 7 ff.

[1186] 1 Cor. ii. 10.

[1187] 1 Cor. ii. 11.

[1188] Jer. xvii. 10.

[1189] Heb. iv. 12.

[1190] 1 Cor. ii. 12, 13.

Chapter XII.

After proof that the Spirit is the Giver of revelation equally with the Father and the Son, it is explained how the same Spirit does not speak of Himself; and it is shown that no bodily organs are to be thought of in Him, and that no inferiority is to be supposed from the fact of our reading that He hears, since the same would have to be attributed to the Son, and indeed even to the Father, since He hears the Son. The Spirit then hears and glorifies the Son in the sense that He revealed Him to the prophets and apostles, by which the Unity of operation of the Three Persons is inferred; and, since the Spirit does the same works as the Father, the substance of each is also declared to be the same.

130. It has then been proved that like as God has revealed to us the things which are His, so too the Son, and so too the Spirit, has revealed the things of God. For our knowledge proceeds from one Spirit, through one Son to one Father; and from one Father through one Son to one Holy Spirit is delivered goodness and sanctification and the sovereign right of eternal power. Where, then, there is a manifestation of the Spirit, there is the power of God, nor can there be any distinction where the work is one. And therefore that which the Son says the Father also says, and that which the Father says the Son also says, and that which the Father and the Son say the Holy Spirit also says.

131. Whence also the Son of God said concerning the Holy Spirit: "He shall not speak from Himself," [1191] that is, not without the participation of the Father and Myself. For the Spirit is not divided and separated, but speaks what He hears. He hears, that is to say, by unity of substance and by the property of knowledge. For He receives not hearing by any orifices of the body, nor does the divine voice resound with any carnal measures, nor does He hear what He knows not; since commonly in human matters hearing produces knowledge, and yet not even in men themselves is there always bodily speech or fleshly hearing. For "he that speaketh in tongues," it is said, "speaketh not to men but to God, for no one heareth, but in the Spirit he speaketh mysteries." [1192]

132. Therefore if in men hearing is not always of the body, do you require in God the voices of man's weakness, and certain organs of fleshly hearing, when He is said to hear in order that we may believe that He knows? For we know that which we have heard, and we hear beforehand that we may be able to know; but in God Who knows all things knowledge goes before hearing. So in order to state that the Son is not ignorant of what the Father wills, we say that He has heard; but in God there is no sound nor syllable, such as usually signify the indication of the will; but oneness of will is comprehended in hidden ways in God, but in us is shown by signs.

133. What means, then, "He shall not speak from Himself"? This is, He shall not speak without Me; for He speaks the truth, He breathes wisdom. He speaks not without the Father, for He is the Spirit of God; He hears not from Himself, for all things are of God.

134. The Son received all things from the Father, for He Himself said: "All things have been delivered unto Me from My Father." [1193] All that is the Father's the Son also has, for He says again: "All things which the Father hath are Mine." [1194] And those things which He Himself received by Unity of nature, the Spirit by the same Unity of nature received also from Him, as the Lord Jesus Himself declares, when speaking of His Spirit: "Therefore said I, He shall receive of Mine and shall declare it unto you." [1195] Therefore what the Spirit says is the Son's, what the Son hath given is the Father's. So neither the Son nor the Spirit speaks anything of Himself. For the Trinity speaks nothing external to Itself.

135. But if you contend that this is an argument for the weakness of the Holy Spirit, and for a kind of likeness to the lowliness of the body, you will also make it an argument to the injury of the Son, because the Son said of Himself: "As I hear I judge," [1196] and "The Son can do nothing else than what He seeth the Father doing." [1197] For if that be true, as it is, which the Son said: "All things which the Father hath are Mine," [1198] and the Son according to the Godhead is One with the Father, One by natural substance, not according to the Sabellian [1199] falsehood; that which is one by the property of substance certainly cannot be separated, and so the Son cannot do anything except what He has heard of the Father, for the Word of God endures forever, [1200] nor is the Father ever separated from the operation of the Son; and that which the Son works He knows that the Father wills, and what the Father wills the Son knows how to work.

136. Lastly, that one may not think that there is any difference of work either in time or in order between the Father and the Son, but may believe the oneness of the same operation, He

says: "The works which I do He doeth." [1201] And again, that one may not think that there is any difference in the distinction of the works, but may judge that the will, the working, and the power of the Father and the Son are the same, Wisdom says concerning the Father: "For whatsoever things He doeth, the Son likewise doeth the same." [1202] So that the action of neither Person is before or after that of the Other, but the same result of one operation. And for this reason the Son says that He can do nothing of Himself, because His operation cannot be separated from that of the Father. In like manner the operation of the Holy Spirit is not separated. Whence also the things which He speaks, He is said to hear from the Father.

137. What if I demonstrate that the Father also hears the Son, as the Son too hears the Father? For you have it written in the Gospel that the Son says: "Father, I thank Thee that Thou heardest Me." [1203] How did the Father hear the Son, since in the previous passage concerning Lazarus the Son spoke nothing to the Father? And that we might not think that the Son was heard once by the Father, He added: "And I knew that Thou hearest Me always." [1204] Therefore the hearing is not that of subject obedience, but of eternal Unity.

138. In like manner, then, the Spirit is said to hear from the Father, and to glorify the Son. To glorify, because the Holy Spirit taught us that the Son is the Image of the invisible God, [1205] and the brightness of His glory, and the impress of His substance. [1206] The Spirit also spoke in the patriarchs and the prophets, and, lastly, the apostles began then to be more perfect after that they had received the Holy Spirit. There is therefore no separation of the divine power and grace, for although "there are diversities of gifts, yet it is the same Spirit; and diversities of ministrations, yet the same Lord; and

diversities of operations, yet the same God Who worketh all in all." [1207] There are diversities of offices, not severances of the Trinity.

139. Lastly, it is the same God Who worketh all in all, that you may know that there is no diversity of operation between God the Father and the Holy Spirit; since those things which the Spirit works, God the Father also works, "Who worketh all in all." For while God the Father worketh all in all, yet "to one is given through the Spirit the word of wisdom; to another the word of knowledge, according to the same Spirit; to another faith, in the same Spirit; to another the gift of healings, in the one Spirit; to another the working of miracles; to another prophecy; to another discerning of spirits; to another divers kinds of tongues; to another the interpretation of sayings; but all these worketh one and the same Spirit, dividing to each one as He will." [1208]

140. There is then no doubt but that those things which the Father worketh, the Spirit worketh also. Nor does He work in accordance with a command, as he who hears in bodily fashion, but voluntarily, as being free in His own will, not the servant of the power of another. For He does not obey as being bidden, but as the giver He is the controller of His own gifts.

141. Consider meanwhile whether you can say that the Spirit effects all things which the Father effects; for you cannot deny that the Father effects those things which the Holy Spirit effects; otherwise the Father does not effect all things, if He effects not those things which the Spirit also effects. But if the Father also effects those things which the Spirit effects, since the Spirit divides His operations, according to His own will, you must of necessity say, either that what the Spirit divides He

divides according to His own will, against the will of God the Father; or if you say that the Father wills the same that the Holy Spirit wills, you must of necessity confess the oneness of the divine will and operation, even if you do it unwillingly, and, if not with the heart, at least with the mouth.

142. But if the Holy Spirit is of one will and operation with God the Father, He is also of one substance, since the Creator is known by His works. So, then, it is the same Spirit, he says, the same Lord, the same God. [1209] And if you say Spirit, He is the same; and if you say Lord, He is the same; and if you say God, He is the same. Not the same, so that Himself is Father, Himself Son, Himself Spirit [one and the selfsame Person]; but because both the Father and the Son are the same Power. He is, then, the same in substance and in power, for there is not in the Godhead either the confusion of Sabellius nor the division of Arius, nor any earthly and bodily change.

[1191] S. John xvi. 13.

[1192] 1 Cor. xiv. 2.

[1193] S. Matt. xi. 27.

[1194] S. John xv. 15.

[1195] S. John xv. 15.

[1196] S. John v. 30.

[1197] S. John v. 19.

[1198] S. John xvi. 15.

[1199] Sabellianism denied the doctrine of the Trinity, maintaining that God is One Person only, manifesting Himself in three characters. See Dict. Chr. Biog. art. "Sabellius," and Blunt, Dict of Sects, etc.

[1200] Ps. cxix. [cxviii.] 89.

[1201] Either S. John v. 17 modified, or a reminiscence of v. 19.

[1202] S. John v. 19.

[1203] S. John xi. 41.

[1204] S. John xi. 42.

[1205] Col. i. 15.

[1206] Heb. i. 3.

[1207] 1 Cor. xii. 4, 5, 6.

[1208] 1 Cor. xii. 8 ff.

[1209] 1 Cor. xii. 5.

Chapter XIII.

Prophecy was not only from the Father and the Son but also from the Spirit; the authority and operation of the latter on the apostles is signified to be the same as Theirs; and so we are to understand that there is unity in the three points of authority, rule, and bounty; yet need no disadvantage be feared from that participation, since such does not arise in human friendship. Lastly, it is established that this is the inheritance of the apostolic faith from the fact that the apostles are described as having obeyed the Holy Spirit.

143. Take, O sacred Emperor, another strong instance in this question, and one known to you: "In many ways and in divers manners, God spake to the fathers in the prophets." [1210] And the Wisdom of God said: "I will send prophets and apostles." [1211] And "To one is given," as it is written, "through the Spirit, the word of wisdom; to another, the word of knowledge, according to the same Spirit; to another faith, in the same Spirit; to another, the gift of healings, in the one Spirit; to another, the working of miracles; to another, prophecy." [1212] Therefore, according to the Apostle, prophecy is not only through the Father and the Son, but also through the Holy Spirit, and therefore the office is one, and the grace one. So you find that the Spirit also is the author of prophecies.

144. The apostles also said: "It seemed good to the Holy Spirit and to us." [1213] And when they say, "It seemed good," they point out not only the Worker of the grace, but also the Author of the carrying out of that which was commanded. For as we read of God: "It pleased God;" so, too, when it is said that, "It

seemed good to the Holy Spirit," one who is master of his own power is portrayed.

145. And how should He not be a master Who speaks what He wills, and commands what He wills, as the Father commands and the Son commands? For as Paul heard the voice saying to him, "I am Jesus, Whom thou persecutest," [1214] so, too, the Spirit forbade Paul and Silas to go into Bithynia. And as the Father spake through the prophets, so, too, Agabus says concerning the Spirit: "Thus saith the Holy Spirit, Thus shall the Jews in Jerusalem bind the man, whose is this girdle." [1215] And as Wisdom sent the apostles, saying, "Go ye into all the world and preach the Gospel," [1216] so, too, the Holy Spirit says: "Separate Me Barnabas and Saul for the work whereunto I have called them." [1217] And so being sent forth by the Holy Spirit, as the Scripture points out farther on, they were distinguished in nothing from the other apostles, as though they were sent in one way by God the Father, in another way by Spirit.

146. Lastly, Paul having been sent by the Spirit, was both a vessel of election on Christ's part, and himself relates that God wrought in him, saying: "For He that wrought for Peter unto the apostleship of the circumcision, wrought for me also unto the Gentiles." [1218] Since, then, the Same wrought in Paul Who wrought in Peter, it is certainly evident that, since the Spirit wrought in Paul, the Holy Spirit wrought also in Peter. But Peter himself testifies that God the Father wrought in him, as it is stated in the Acts of the Apostles that Peter rose up and said to them: "Men and brethren, ye know that a good while ago God made choice amongst us that the Gentiles should hear the word of the Gospel from my mouth." See, then, in Peter God wrought the grace of preaching. And who would dare to

deny the operation of Christ in him, since he was certainly elected and chosen by Christ, when the Lord said: "Feed My lambs." [1219]

147. The operation, then, of the Father, the Son, and the Holy Spirit is one, unless perchance you, who deny the oneness of the same operation upon the Apostle, think this; that the Father and the Spirit wrought in Peter, in whom the Son had wrought, as if the operation of the Son by no means sufficed for him to the attainment of the grace. And so the strength of the Father, of the Son, and of the Holy Spirit being as it were joined and brought together, the work was manifold, lest the operation of Christ alone should be too weak to establish Peter.

148. And not only in Peter is there found to be one operation of the Father, the Son, and the Holy Spirit, but also in all the apostles the unity of the divine operation, and a certain authority over the dispensations of heaven. For the divine operation works by the power of a command, not in the execution of a ministry; for God, when He works, does not fashion anything by toil or art, but "He spake and they were made." [1220] He said, "Let there be light, and there was light," [1221] for the effecting of the work is comprised in the commandment of God.

149. We can, then, easily find, if we will consider, that this royal power is by the witness of the Scriptures attributed to the Holy Spirit; and it will be made clear that all the apostles were not only disciples of Christ, but also ministers of the Father, the Son, and the Holy Spirit. As also the teacher of the Gentiles tells us, when he says: "God hath set some in the Church, first apostles, secondarily prophets, thirdly teachers; then miracles,

162

the gift of healings, helps, governments, divers kinds of tongues." [1222]

150. See, God set apostles, and set prophets and teachers, gave the gift of healings, which you find above to be given by the Holy Spirit; gave divers kinds of tongues. But yet all are not apostles, all are not prophets, all are not teachers. Not all, says he, have the gift of healings, nor do all, says he, speak with tongues. [1223] For the whole of the divine gifts cannot exist in each several man; each, according to his capacity, receives that which he either desires or deserves. But the power of the Trinity, which is lavish of all graces, is not like this weakness.

151. Lastly, God set apostles. Those whom God set in the Church, Christ chose and ordained to be apostles, and sent them into the world, saying: "Go ye into all the world, and preach the Gospel to the whole creation. He that shall believe and be baptized shall be saved, but he that believeth not shall be damned. And these signs shall follow them that believe. In My Name shall they cast out devils, they shall speak with new tongues, they shall take up serpents, and if they shall drink any deadly thing, it shall not hurt them, they shall lay hands on the sick, and they shall recover." [1224] You see the Father and Christ also set teachers in the Churches; and as the Father gives the gift of healings, so, too, does the Son give; as the Father gives the gift of tongues, so, too, has the Son also granted it.

152. In like manner we have heard also above concerning the Holy Spirit, that He too grants the same kinds of graces. For it is said: "To one is given through the Spirit the gift of healings, to another divers kinds of tongues, to another prophecy." [1225] So, then, the Spirit gives the same gifts as the Father, and the Son also gives them. Let us now learn more expressly

what we have touched upon above, that the Holy Spirit entrusts the same office as the Father and the Son, and appoints the same persons; since Paul said: "Take heed to yourselves, and to all the flock in the which the Holy Spirit has made you overseers to rule the Church of God." [1226]

153. There is, then, unity of authority, unity of appointment, unity of giving. For if you separate appointment and power, what cause was there [for maintaining] that those whom Christ appointed as apostles, God the Father appointed, and the Holy Spirit appointed? unless, perhaps, as if sharing a possession or a right, They, like men, were afraid of legal prejudice, and therefore the operation was divided, and the authority distributed.

154. These things are narrow and paltry, even between men, who for the most part, although they do not agree in action, yet agree in will. So that a certain person being asked what a friend is, answered, "A second self." If, then, a man so defined a friend as to say, he was a second self, that is to say, through a oneness of love and good-will, how much more ought we to esteem the oneness of Majesty, in the Father, the Son, and the Holy Ghost, when by the same operation and divine power, either the unity, or certainly that which is more, the tautotes, as it is called in Greek, is expressed, for tauto signifies "the same," so that the Father, the Son, and the Holy Spirit have the same; so that to have the same will and the same power does not arise from the affection of the will, but inheres in the substance of the Trinity.

155. This is the inheritance of apostolic faith and devotion, which one may observe also in the Acts of the Apostles. Therefore Paul and Barnabas obeyed the commands of the

Holy Spirit. And all the apostles obeyed, and forthwith ordained those whom the Spirit had ordered to be separated: "Separate Me," said He, "Barnabas and Saul." [1227] Do you see the authority of Him Who commands? Consider the merit of those who obey.

156. Paul believed, and because he believed he cast off the zeal of a persecutor, and gained a crown of righteousness. He believed who used to make havoc of the Churches; but being converted to the faith, he preached in the Spirit that which the Spirit commanded. [1228] The Spirit anointed His champion, and having shaken off the dust of unbelief, presented him as an insuperable conqueror of the unbelievers to various assemblies of the ungodly, and trained him by many sufferings for the prize of his high calling in Christ Jesus.

157. Barnabas also believed, and obeyed because he believed. Therefore, being chosen by the authority of the Holy Spirit, Which came on him abundantly, as a special sign of his merits, he was not unworthy of so great a fellowship. For one grace shone in these whom one Spirit had chosen.

158. Nor was Paul inferior to Peter, though the latter was the foundation of the Church, and the former a wise builder knowing how to make firm the footsteps of the nations who believed; Paul was not, I say, unworthy of the fellowship of the apostles, but is easily comparable with the first, and second to none. For he who knows not that he is inferior makes himself equal.

[1210] Heb. i. 1.

[1211] S. Luke xi. 49.

[1212] 1 Cor. xii. 8, 9, 10.

[1213] Acts xv. 28.

[1214] Acts ix. 5.

[1215] Acts xxi. 11.

[1216] S. Mark xvi. 15.

[1217] Acts xiii. 2.

[1218] Gal. ii. 8.

[1219] S. John xxi. 15.

[1220] Ps. xxxiii. [xxxii.] 9.

[1221] Gen. i. 3.

[1222] 1 Cor. xii. 28.

[1223] 1 Cor. xii. 30.

[1224] S. Mark xvi. 15 ff.

[1225] 1 Cor. xii. 8, 9.

[1226] Acts xx. 28.

[1227] Acts xiii. 2.

[1228] Acts ix. 20.

Book III.

Chapter I.

Not only were the prophets and apostles sent by the Spirit, but also the Son of God. This is proved from Isaiah and the evangelists, and it is explained why St. Luke wrote that the same Spirit descended like a dove upon Christ and abode upon Him. Next, after establishing this mission of Christ, the writer infers that the Son is sent by the Father and the Spirit, as the Spirit is by the Father and the Son.

1. In the former book [1229] we have shown by the clear evidence of the Scriptures that the apostles and prophets were appointed, the latter to prophesy, the former to preach the Gospel, by the Holy Spirit in the same way as by the Father and the Son; now we add what all will rightly wonder at, and not be able to doubt, that the Spirit was upon Christ; and that as He sent the Spirit, so the Spirit sent the Son of God. For the Son of God says: "The Spirit of the Lord is upon Me, because He hath anointed Me, He hath sent Me to preach the Gospel to the poor, to proclaim liberty to the captives, and sight to the blind." [1230] And having read this from the Book of Isaiah, He says in the Gospel: "To-day hath this Scripture been fulfilled in your ears;" [1231] that He might point out that it was said of Himself.

2. Can we, then, wonder if the Spirit sent both the prophets and the apostles, since Christ said: "The Spirit of the Lord is upon Me"? And rightly did He say "upon Me," because He was speaking as the Son of Man. For as the Son of Man He was anointed and sent to preach the Gospel.

3. But if they believe not the Son, let them hear the Father also saying that the Spirit of the Lord is upon Christ. For He says to John: "Upon whomsoever thou shalt see the Spirit descending from heaven and abiding upon Him, He it is Who baptizeth with the Holy Spirit." [1232] God the Father said this to John, and John heard and saw and believed. He heard from God, he saw in the Lord, he believed that it was the Spirit Who was coming down from heaven. For it was not a dove that descended, but the Holy Spirit as a dove; for thus it is written: "I saw the Spirit descending from heaven as a dove." [1233]

4. As John says that he saw, so, too, wrote Mark; Luke, however, added that the Holy Spirit descended in a bodily form as a dove; you must not think that this was an incarnation, but an appearance. He, then, brought the appearance before him, that by means of the appearance he might believe who did not see the Spirit, and that by the appearance He might manifest that He had a share of the one honour in authority, the one operation in the mystery, the one gift in the bath, together with the Father and the Son; unless perchance we consider Him in Whom the Lord was baptized too weak for the servant to be baptized in Him.

5. And he said fittingly, "abiding upon Him," [1234] because the Spirit inspired a saying or acted upon the prophets as often as He would, but abode always in Christ.

6. Nor, again, let it move you that he said "upon Him," for he was speaking of the Son of Man, because he was baptized as the Son of Man. For the Spirit is not upon Christ, according to the Godhead, but in Christ; for, as the Father is in the Son, and the Son in the Father, so the Spirit of God and the Spirit of Christ is both in the Father and in the Son, for He is the Spirit

of His mouth. For He Who is of God abides in God, as it is written: "But we received not the spirit of this world, but the Spirit which is of God." [1235] And He abides in Christ, Who has received from Christ; for it is written again: "He shall take of Mine:" [1236] and elsewhere: "The law of the Spirit of life in Christ Jesus made me free from the law of sin and death." [1237] He is, then, not over Christ according to the Godhead of Christ, for the Trinity is not over Itself, but over all things: It is not over Itself but in Itself.

7. Who, then, can doubt that the Spirit sent the prophets and apostles, since the Son of God says: "The Spirit of the Lord is upon Me." [1238] And elsewhere: "I am the First, and I am also for ever, and Mine hand hath founded the earth, and My right hand hath established the heaven; I will call them and they shall stand up together, and shall all be gathered together and shall hear. Who hath declared these things to them? Because I loved thee I performed thy pleasure against Babylon, that the seed of the Chaldaeans might be taken away. I have spoken, and I have called, I have brought him and have made his way prosperous. Come unto Me and hear ye this. From the beginning I have not spoken in secret, I was there when those things were done; and now the Lord God hath sent Me and His Spirit." [1239] Who is it Who says: The Lord God hath sent Me and His Spirit, except He Who came from the Father that He might save sinners? And, as you hear, the Spirit sent Him, lest when you hear that the Son sends the Spirit, you should believe the Spirit to be of inferior power.

8. So both the Father and the Spirit sent the Son; the Father sent Him, for it is written: "But the Paraclete, the Holy Spirit, Whom the Father will send in My Name." [1240] The Son sent Him, for He said: "But when the Paraclete is come, Whom I

will send unto you from the Father, even the Spirit of Truth."
[1241] If, then, the Son and the Spirit send each other, as the
Father sends, there is no inferiority of subjection, but a
community of power.

[1229] Bk. II. 12.

[1230] Isa. lxi. 1 [LXX.].

[1231] S. Luke iv. 21.

[1232] S. John i. 33.

[1233] S. John i. 32.

[1234] S. John i. 33.

[1235] 1 Cor. ii. 12.

[1236] S. John xvi. 14.

[1237] Rom. viii. 2.

[1238] S. Luke iv. 18.

[1239] Isa. xlii. 12 ff. [LXX.].

[1240] S. John xiv. 26.

[1241] S. John xv. 26.

Chapter II.
**The Son and the Spirit are alike given; whence not
subjection but one Godhead is shown by Its working.**

9. And not only did the Father send the Son, but also gave
Him, as the Son Himself gave Himself. For we read: "Grace to

you from God our Father and the Lord Jesus Christ, Who gave Himself for our sins." [1242] If they think that He was subject in that He was sent, they cannot deny that it was of grace that He was given. But He was given by the Father, as Isaiah said: "Unto us a Child is born, unto us a Son is given;" [1243] but He was given, I dare to say it, by the Spirit also, Who was sent by the Spirit. For since the prophet has not defined by whom He was given, he shows that He was given by the grace of the Trinity; and inasmuch as the Son Himself gave Himself, He could not be subject to Himself according to His Godhead. Therefore that He was given could not be a sign of subjection in the God-head.

10. But the Holy Spirit also was given, for it is written: "I will ask the Father, and He shall give you another Paraclete." [1244] And the Apostle says: "Wherefore he that despiseth these things despiseth not man but God, Who hath given us His Holy Spirit." [1245] Isaiah, too, shows that both the Spirit and the Son are given: "Thus," says he, "saith the Lord God, Who made the heaven and fashioned it, Who stablished the earth, and the things which are in it, and giveth breath to the people upon it, and the Spirit to them that walk upon it." [1246] And to the Son: "I am the Lord God, Who have called Thee in righteousness, and will hold Thine hand, and will strengthen Thee; and I have given Thee for a covenant of My people, for a light of the Gentiles, to open the eyes of the blind, to bring out of their fetters those that are bound." [1247] Since, then, the Son is both sent and given, and the Spirit also is both sent and given, They have assuredly a oneness of Godhead Who have a oneness of action.

[1242] Gal. i. 3, 4.

171

[1243] Isa. ix. 6.

[1244] S. John xiv. 16.

[1245] 1 Thess. iv. 8.

[1246] Isa. xlii. 5.

[1247] Isa. xlii. 6, 7.

Chapter III.

The same Unity may also be recognized from the fact that the Spirit is called Finger, and the Son Right Hand; for the understanding of divine things is assisted by the usage of human language. The tables of the law were written by this Finger, and they were afterwards broken, and the reason. Lastly, Christ wrote with the same Finger; yet we must not admit any inferiority in the Spirit from this bodily comparison.

11. So, too, the Spirit is also called the Finger of God, because there is an indivisible and inseparable communion between the Father, the Son, and the Holy Spirit. For as the Scripture called the Son of God the Right Hand of God, as it is said: "Thy Right Hand, O Lord, is made glorious in power. Thy Right Hand, O Lord, hath dashed in pieces the enemy;" [1248] so the Holy Spirit is called the Finger of God, as the Lord Himself says: "But if I by the Finger of God cast out devils." [1249] For in the same place in another book of the Gospel He named the Spirit of God, as you find: "But if I by the Spirit of God cast out devils." [1250]

12. What, then, could have been said to signify more expressly the unity of the Godhead, or of Its working, which Unity is according to the Godhead of the Father, or of the Son, or of

the Holy Spirit, than that we should understand that the fulness of the eternal Godhead would seem to be divided far more than this body of ours, if any one were to sever the unity of Substance, and multiply Its powers, whereas the eternity of the same Godhead is one?

13. For oftentimes it is convenient to estimate from our own words those things which are above us, and because we cannot see those things we draw inferences from those which we can see. "For the invisible things of Him," says the Apostle, "from the creation of the world are clearly seen, being understood by those things which are made." [1251] And he adds: "His eternal power also and Godhead." [1252] Of which one thing seems to be said of the Son, and another of the Holy Spirit; that in the same manner as the Son is called the eternal Power of the Father, so, also, the Spirit, because He is divine, should be believed to be His eternal Godhead. For the Son, too, because He ever lives, is eternal life. This Finger, then, of God is both eternal and divine. For what is there belonging to God which is not eternal and divine?

14. With this Finger, as we read, God wrote on those tables of stone which Moses received. For God did not with a finger of flesh write the forms and portions of those letters which we read, but gave the law by His Spirit. And so the Apostle says: "For the Law is spiritual, which, indeed, is written not with ink, but with the Spirit of the living God; not in tables of stone, but on fleshy tables of the heart." [1253] For if the letter of the Apostle is written in the Spirit, what hinders us from believing that the Law of God was written not with ink, but with the Spirit of God, which certainly does not stain but enlightens the secret places of our heart and mind?

14. Now it was written on tables of stone, because it was written in a type, but the tables were first broken and cast out of the hands of Moses, because the Jews fell away from the works of the prophet. And fitly were the tables broken, not the writing erased. And do you see that your table be not broken, that your mind and soul be not divided. Is Christ divided? He is not divided, but is one with the Father; and let no one separate you from Him. If your faith fails, the table of your heart is broken. The coherence of your soul is lessened if you do not believe the unity of Godhead in the Trinity. Your faith is written, and your sin is written, as Jeremiah said: "Thy sin, O Judah, is written with a pen of iron and the point of a diamond. And it is written," he says, "on thy breast and on thy heart." [1254] The sin, therefore, is there where grace is, but the sin is written with a pen, grace is denoted by the Spirit.

15. With this Finger, also, the Lord Jesus, with bowed head, mystically wrote on the ground, when the adulteress was brought before Him by the Jews, signifying in a figure that, when we judge of the sins of another, we ought to remember our own.

16. And lest, again, because God wrote the Law by His Spirit, we should believe any inferiority, as it were, concerning the ministry of the Spirit, or from the consideration of our own body should think the Spirit to be a small part of God, the Apostle says, elsewhere, that he does not speak with words of human wisdom, but in words taught by the Spirit, and that he compares spiritual things with spiritual; but that the natural man receiveth not the things which pertain to the Spirit of God. [1255] For he knew that he who compared divine with carnal things was amongst natural things, and not to be reckoned amongst spiritual men; "for they are foolishness," he

174

says, "unto him." [1256] And so, because he knew that these questions would arise amongst natural men, foreseeing the future he says: "For who hath known the mind of the Lord, that he may instruct Him? But we have the mind of Christ." [1257]

[1248] Ex. xv. 6.

[1249] S. Luke xi. 20.

[1250] S. Matt. xii. 28.

[1251] Rom. i. 20.

[1252] Rom. i. 20.

[1253] 2 Cor. iii. 3.

[1254] Jer. xvii. 1.

[1255] 1 Cor. ii. 13, 14.

[1256] 1 Cor. ii. 13, 14.

[1257] 1 Cor. ii. 16.

Chapter IV.

To those who contend that the Spirit because He is called the Finger is less than the Father, St. Ambrose replies that this would also tend to the lessening of the Son, Who is called the Right Hand. That these names are to be referred only to the Unity, for which reason Moses proclaimed that the whole Trinity worked in the passage of the Red Sea. And, indeed, it is no wonder that the operation of the Spirit found place there, where there was a figure of baptism, since the Scripture teaches that the

Three Persons equally sanctify and are operative in that sacrament.

17. But if any one is still entangled in carnal doubts, and hesitates because of bodily figures, let him consider that he cannot think rightly of the Son who can think wrongly of the Spirit. For if some think that the Spirit is a certain small portion of God, because He is called the Finger of God, the same persons must certainly maintain that a small portion only is in the Son of God, because He is called the Right Hand of God.

18. But the Son is called both the Right Hand and the Power of God; if, then, we consider our words, there can be no perfection without power; let them therefore take care lest they think that which it is impious to say, namely, that the Father being but half perfect in His own Substance received perfection through the Son, and let them cease to deny that the Son is co-eternal with the Father. For when did the Power of God not exist? But if they think that at any time the Power of God existed not, they will say that at some time Perfection existed not in God the Father, to Whom they think that Power was at some time wanting.

19. But, as I said, these things are written that we may refer them to the Unity of the Godhead, and believe that which the Apostle said, that the fulness of the Godhead dwells bodily in Christ, [1258] which dwells also in the Father, and dwells in the Holy Spirit; and that, as there is a unity of the Godhead, so also is there a unity of operation.

20. And this may also be gathered from the Song of Moses, for he, after leading the people of the Jews through the sea, acknowledged the operation of the Father, the Son, and the Holy Spirit, saying: "Thy Right Hand, O Lord, is glorious in

power, Thy Right Hand, O Lord, hath dashed in pieces the enemy." [1259] Here you have his confession of the Son and of the Father, Whose Right Hand He is. And farther on, not to pass by the Holy Spirit, He added: "Thou didst send Thy Spirit and the sea covered them, and the water was divided by the Spirit of Thine anger." [1260] By which is signified the unity of the Godhead, not an inequality of the Trinity.

21. You see, then, that the Holy Spirit also co-operated with the Father and the Son, so that just as if the waves were congealed in the midst of the sea, a wall as it were of water rose up for the passage of the Jews, and then, poured back again by the Spirit, overwhelmed the people of the Egyptians. And many think that from the same origin the pillar of cloud went before the people of the Jews by day, and the pillar of fire by night, that the grace of the Spirit might protect His people.

22. Now that this operation of God, which the whole world rightly wonders at, did not take place without the work of the Holy Spirit, the Apostle also declared when he said that the truth of a spiritual mystery was prefigured in it, for we read as follows: "For our fathers were all under the cloud, and all passed through the sea, and were all baptized in Moses in the cloud and in the sea, and did all eat the same spiritual meat, and did all drink the same spiritual drink." [1261]

23. For how without the operation of the Holy Spirit could there be the type of a sacrament, the whole truth of which is in the Spirit? As the Apostle also set forth, saying: "But ye were washed, but ye were sanctified, but ye were justified in the Name of our Lord Jesus Christ, and in the Spirit of our God." [1262]

24. You see, then, that the Father works in the Son, and that the Son works in the Spirit. And therefore do not doubt that, according to the order of Scripture, there was in the figure that which the Truth Himself declared to be in the truth. For who can deny His operation in the Font, in which we feel His operation and grace?

25. For as the Father sanctifies, so, too, the Son sanctifies, and the Holy Spirit sanctifies. The Father sanctifies according to that which is written: "The God of peace sanctify you, and may your spirit, soul, and body be preserved entire without blame in the day of our Lord Jesus Christ." [1263] And elsewhere the Son says: "Father, sanctify them in the truth." [1264]

26. But of the Son the same Apostle said: "Who was made unto us wisdom from God, and righteousness, and sanctification, and redemption." [1265] Do you see that He was made sanctification? But He was made so unto us, not that He should change that which He was, but that He might sanctify us in the flesh.

27. And the Apostle also teaches that the Holy Spirit sanctifies. For he speaks thus: "We are bound to give thanks to God always for you, brethren dearly beloved of the Lord; because God chose you as first-fruits unto salvation, in sanctification of the Spirit, and belief of the truth." [1266]

28. So, then, the Father sanctifies, the Son also sanctifies, and the Holy Spirit sanctifies; but the sanctification is one, for baptism is one, and the grace of the sacrament is one.

[1258] Col. ii. 9.

[1259] Ex. xv. 6.

[1260] Ex. xv. 10.

[1261] 1 Cor. x. 1, 2, 3, 4.

[1262] 1 Cor. vi. 11.

[1263] 1 Thess. v. 23.

[1264] S. John xvii. 17.

[1265] 1 Cor. i. 30.

[1266] 2 Thess. ii. 13.

Chapter V.
The writer sums up the argument he had commenced, and confirms the statement that unity is signified by the terms finger and right hand, from the fact that the works of God are the same as are the works of hands; and that those of hands are the same as those of fingers; and lastly, that the term hand applies equally to the Son and the Spirit, and that of finger applies to the Spirit and the Son.

29. But what wonder is it if He Who Himself needs no sanctification, but abounds therewith, sanctifies each man; since, as I said, we have been taught that His Majesty is so great, that the Holy Spirit seems to be as inseparable from God the Father as the finger is from the body?

30. But if any one thinks that this should be referred not to the oneness of power, but to its lessening, he indeed will fall into such madness as to appear to fashion the Father, Son, and Holy Spirit as it were into one bodily form, and to picture to himself certain distinctions of its members.

31. But let them learn, as I have often said, that not inequality but unity of power is signified by this testimony; inasmuch as things which are the works of God are also the works of hands, and we read that the same are the works of fingers. For it is written: "The heavens declare the glory of God, and the firmament showeth the work of His hands;" [1267] and elsewhere: "In the beginning Thou didst found the earth, O Lord; and the heavens are the works of Thy hands." [1268] So, then, the works of the hands are the same as the works of God. There is not therefore any distinction of the work according to the kind of bodily members, but a oneness of power.

32. But those which are the works of the hands are also the works of the fingers, for it is equally written: "For I will behold Thy heavens, the works of Thy fingers, the moon, and the stars, which Thou hast established." [1269] What less are the fingers here said to have made than the hands, since they made the same as the hands, as it is written: "For Thou, Lord, hast made me glad through Thy work, and in the works of Thy hands will I rejoice." [1270]

33. And yet since we read that the Son is the hand (for it is written: "Hath not My Hand made all these things?" [1271] and elsewhere: "I will place thee in the cleft of the rock, and I will cover thee with Mine hand, I have placed My hand under the covering of the rock," [1272] which refers to the mystery of the Incarnation, because the eternal Power of God took on Itself the covering of a body), it is certainly clear that Scripture used the term hand both of the Son and of the Holy Spirit.

34. And again, since we read that the Spirit is the finger of God, we think that fingers [in the plural] are spoken of to signify the Son and Spirit. Lastly, that he may state that he received the

sanctification both of the Son and of the Spirit, a certain saint says: "Thy hands have made me and fashioned me." [1273]

[1267] Ps. xix. [xviii.] 1.

[1268] Ps. cii. [ci.] 26.

[1269] Ps. viii. 3.

[1270] Ps. xcii. [xci.] 4.

[1271] Isa. lxvi. 2.

[1272] Ex. xxxiii. 22.

[1273] Ps. cxix. [cxviii.] 73.

Chapter VI.
The Spirit rebukes just as do the Father and the Son; and indeed judges could not judge without Him, as is shown by the judgments of Solomon and Daniel, which are explained in a few words, by the way; and no other than the Holy Spirit inspired Daniel.

35. Why do we reject like words when we assert the oneness of power, since the oneness of power extends so far that the Spirit rebukes, as the Father rebukes, and as the Son rebukes. For so it is written: "O Lord, rebuke me not in Thine anger, neither chasten me in Thy displeasure." [1274] Then in the forty-ninth [fiftieth] Psalm, the Lord speaks thus: "I will rebuke thee, and will set thy sins before thy face." [1275] And in like manner the Son said of the Holy Spirit: "When I go away, I will send the Paraclete to you. And He, when He is come, will rebuke the world, concerning sin, and concerning righteousness, and concerning judgment." [1276]

36. But whither is the madness of faithless men leading us, so that we appear to be proving, as if it were a matter of doubt, that the Holy Spirit rebukes, whereas judges themselves are unable to judge, except through the Spirit. Lastly, that famous judgment of Solomon, when, amongst the difficulties arising from those who were contending, as one, having overlain the child which she had borne, wished to claim the child of another, and the other was protecting her own son, he both discovered deceit in the very hidden thoughts, and affection in the mother's heart, was certainly so admirable only by the gift of the Holy Spirit. For no other sword would have penetrated the hidden feeling of those women, except the sword of the Spirit, of which the Lord says: "I am not come to send peace but a sword." [1277] For the inmost mind cannot be penetrated by steel, but by the Spirit: "For the Spirit of understanding is holy, one only, manifold, subtle, lively," and, farther on, "overseeing all things." [1278]

37. Consider what the prophet says, that He oversees all things. And so Solomon also oversaw, so that he ordered that sword to be brought, because while pretending that he intended to divide the infant, he reflected that the true mother would have more regard for her son than for her comfort, and would set kindness before right, not right before kindness. But that she who feigned the feelings of a mother, blinded by the desire of gaining her end, would think little of the destruction of him in regard to whom she felt no outgoing of tenderness. And so that spiritual man, that he might judge all things (for he that is spiritual judgeth all things), [1279] sought in the feelings the natural disposition which was concealed in the language, and questioned tenderness that he might set forth the truth. So the

mother overcame by the affection of love, which is a fruit of the Spirit.

38. He judges in a prophet, for the word of wisdom is given by the Spirit; [1280] how, then, do men deny that the Spirit can rebuke the world concerning judgment, Who removes doubt from judgment, and grants the successful issue?

39. Daniel also, unless he had received the Spirit of God, would never have been able to discover that lustful adultery, that fraudulent lie. For when Susanna, assailed by the conspiracy of the elders, saw that the mind of the people was moved by consideration for the old men, and destitute of all help, alone amongst men, conscious of her chastity she prayed God to judge; it is written: "The Lord heard her voice, when she was being led to be put to death, and the Lord raised up the Holy Spirit of a young youth, whose name was Daniel." [1281] And so according to the grace of the Holy Spirit received by him, he discovered the varying evidence of the treacherous, for it was none other than the operation of divine power, that his voice should make them whose inward feelings were concealed to be known.

41. Understand, then, the sacred and heavenly miracle of the Holy Spirit. She who preferred to be chaste in herself, rather than in the opinion of the people, she who preferred to hazard [the reputation of] her innocence, rather than her modesty, who when she was accused was silent, when she was condemned held her peace, content with the judgment of her own conscience, who preserved regard for her modesty even in peril, that they who were not able to force her chastity might not seem to have forced her to petulance; when she called upon

the Lord, she obtained the Spirit, Who made known the hidden consciousness of the elders.

42. Let the chaste learn not to dread calumny. For she who preferred chastity to life did not suffer the loss of life, and retained the glory of chastity. So, too, Abraham, once bidden to go to foreign lands, and not being held back either by the danger to his wife's modesty, nor by the fear of death before him, preserved both his own life and his wife's chastity. [1282] So no one has ever repented of trusting God, and chastity increased devotion in Sarah, and devotion chastity.

43. And lest any one should perhaps think that, as the Scripture says, "God raised up the Holy Spirit of a young youth," the Spirit in him was that of a man, not the Holy Spirit, let him read farther on, and he will find that Daniel received the Holy Spirit, and therefore prophesied. Lastly, too, the king advanced him because he had the grace of the Spirit. For he speaks thus: "Thou, O Daniel, art able, forasmuch as the Holy Spirit of God is in thee." [1283] And farther on it is written: "And Daniel was set over them, because an excellent Spirit was in him." [1284] And the Spirit of Moses also was distributed to those who were to be judges. [1285]

[1274] Ps. vi. 1.

[1275] Ps. l. [xlix.] 21.

[1276] S. John xvi. 7, 8.

[1277] S. Matt. x. 34.

[1278] Wisd. vii. 22, 23.

[1279] 1 Cor. ii. 15.

[1280] 1 Cor. xii. 8.

[1281] Hist. Sus. [Dan. iii.] 44, 45.

[1282] Gen. xx. 1 ff.

[1283] Dan. v. 14.

[1284] Dan. vi. 3.

[1285] Num. xi. 25.

Chapter VII.

The Son Himself does not judge or punish without the Spirit, so that the same Spirit is called the Sword of the Word. But inasmuch as the Word is in turn called the Sword of the Spirit, the highest unity of power is thereby recognized in each.

44. But what should we say of the other points? We have heard that the Lord Jesus not only judges in the Spirit but punishes also. For neither would He punish Antichrist, whom, as we read, "the Lord Jesus shall slay with the Spirit of His mouth," [1286] unless He had before judged of his deserts. Yet here is not a grace received, but the unity remains undivided, since neither can Christ be without the Spirit, nor the Spirit without Christ. For the unity of the divine nature cannot be divided.

45. And since that instance comes before us, that the Lord Jesus shall slay with the Spirit of His mouth, the Spirit is understood to be as it were the Sword of the Word. Lastly, in the Gospel also the Lord Jesus Himself says: "I came not to send peace but a sword." [1287] For He came that He might give the Spirit; and so there is in His mouth a two-edged sword,

[1288] which is in truth the grace of the Spirit. So the Spirit is the Sword of the Word.

46. And that you may know that there is no inequality but unity of nature, the Word also is the Sword of the Holy Spirit, for it is written: "Taking the shield of faith, wherewith ye may be able to quench all the fiery darts of the wicked one. And take the helmet of Salvation, and the sword of the Spirit, which is the Word of God." [1289]

47. Since, then, the Sword of the Word is the Holy Spirit, and the Sword of the Holy Spirit is the Word of God, there is certainly in Them oneness of power.

[1286] 2 Thess. ii. 8.

[1287] S. Matt. x. 34.

[1288] Rev. xix. 15.

[1289] Eph. vi. 16, 17.

Chapter VIII.
The aforesaid unity is proved hereby, that as the Father is said to be grieved and tempted, so too the Son. The Son was also tempted in the wilderness, where a figure of the cross was set up in the brazen serpent: but the Apostle says that the Spirit also was there tempted. St. Ambrose infers from this that the Israelites were guided into the promised land by the same Spirit, and that His will and power are one with those of the Father and the Son.

48. And we may behold this unity also in other passages of the Scriptures. For whereas Ezekiel says to the people of the Jews: "And thou hast grieved Me in all these things, saith the Lord;"

[1290] Paul says to the new people in his Epistle: "Grieve not the Holy Spirit of God, in Whom ye were sealed." [1291] Again, whereas Isaiah says of the Jews themselves: "But they believed not, but grieved the Holy Spirit;" [1292] David says of God: "They grieved the Most High in the desert, and tempted God in their hearts." [1293]

49. Understand also that whereas Scripture in other places says that the Spirit was tempted, and that God was tempted, it says also that Christ was tempted; for you have the Apostle saying to the Corinthians: "Neither let us tempt Christ, as some of them tempted, and perished by serpents." [1294] Just was the punishment that the adversaries should feel the venom, who had not venerated the Maker.

50. And well did the Lord ordain that by the lifting up of the brazen serpent the wounds of those who were bitten should be healed; for the brazen serpent is a type of the Cross; for although in His flesh Christ was lifted up, yet in Him was the Apostle crucified to the world and the world to him; for he says: "The world hath been crucified unto me, and I unto the world." [1295] "So the world was crucified in its allurements, and therefore not a real but a brazen serpent was hanged; because the Lord took on Him the likeness of a sinner, in the truth, indeed, of His Body, but without the truth of sin, that imitating a serpent through the deceitful appearance of human weakness, having laid aside the slough of the flesh, He might destroy the cunning of the true serpent. And therefore in the Cross of the Lord, which came to man's help in avenging temptation, I, who accept the medicine of the Trinity, recognize in the wicked the offence against the Trinity.

51. Therefore when you find in the book of Moses, that the Lord being tempted sent serpents on the people of the Jews, it is necessary that you either confess the Unity of the Father, Son, and Holy Spirit in the Divine Majesty, or certainly when the writing of the Apostle says that the Spirit was tempted, it undoubtedly pointed out the Spirit by the name of Lord. But the Apostle writing to the Hebrews says that the Spirit was tempted, for you find this: "Wherefore the Holy Ghost saith this: Today if ye shall hear His voice, harden not your hearts, like as in the provocation in the day of temptation in the wilderness, where your fathers tempted Me, proved Me, and saw My works. Forty years was I near to this generation and said: They do alway err in their heart; but they did not know My ways, as I sware in My wrath, If they shall enter into My rest." [1296]

52. Therefore, according to the Apostle, the Spirit was tempted. If He was tempted, He also certainly was guiding the people of the Jews into the land of promise, as it is written: "For He led them through the deep, as a horse through the wilderness, and they laboured not, and like the cattle through the plain. The Spirit came down from the Lord and guided them." [1297] And He certainly ministered to them the calm rain of heavenly food, He with fertile shower made fruitful that daily harvest which earth had not brought forth, and husbandman had not sown.

53. Now let us look at these points one by one. God had promised rest to the Jews; the Spirit calls that rest His. God the Father relates that He was tempted by the unbelieving, and the Spirit says that He was tempted by the same, for the temptation is one wherewith the one Godhead of the Trinity was tempted by the unbelieving. God condemns the people of the Jews, so that they cannot attain to the land flowing with milk and honey,

that is, to the rest of the resurrection; and the Spirit condemns them by the same decree: "If they shall enter into My rest." It is, then, the decree of one Will, the excellency of one Power.

[1290] Ezek. xvi. 43.

[1291] Eph. iv. 30.

[1292] Isa. lxiii. 10.

[1293] Ps. lxxviii. [lxvii.] 17, 18.

[1294] 1 Cor. x. 9.

[1295] Gal. vi. 14.

[1296] Heb. iii. 7-11.

[1297] Isa. lxiii. 13, 14.

Chapter IX.
That the Holy Spirit is provoked is proved by the words of St. Peter, in which it is shown that the Spirit of God is one and the same as the Spirit of the Lord, both by other passages and by reference to the sentence of the same Apostle on Ananias and Sapphira, whence it is argued that the union of the Holy Spirit with the Father and the Son, as well as His own Godhead, is proved.

54. Perhaps, however, some one might say that this passage cannot be specially applied to the Holy Spirit, had not the same Apostle Peter taught us in another place that the Holy Ghost can be tempted by our sins, for you find that the wife of Ananias is thus addressed: "Why have ye agreed together to tempt the Spirit of the Lord?" [1298] For the Spirit of the Lord is the very Spirit of God; for there is one Holy Spirit, as also

the Apostle Paul taught, saying: "But ye are not in the flesh, but in the Spirit, if so be that the Spirit of God dwelleth in you. But if any man hath not the Spirit of Christ, he is none of His." [1299] He first mentioned the Spirit of God and immediately adds that the Same is the Spirit of Christ. And having spoken of the Spirit, that we might understand that where the Holy Spirit is there is Christ, he added: "But if Christ be in you." [1300]

55. Then, in the same way as we here understand that where the Spirit is there also is Christ; so also, elsewhere, he shows that where Christ is, there also is the Holy Spirit. For having said: "Do ye seek a proof of Christ Who speaketh in me?" [1301] he says elsewhere: "For I think that I also have the Spirit of God." [1302] The Unity, then, is inseparable, for by the testimony of Scripture where either the Father or the Son or the Holy Spirit is designated, there is all the fulness of the Trinity.

56. But Peter himself in the instance we have brought forward spoke first of the Holy Spirit, and then called Him the Spirit of the Lord, for you read as follows: "Ananias, why hath Satan filled thine heart to lie to the Holy Spirit, and to deal fraudulently concerning the price of the field? While it remained did it not continue thine own, and when sold was it not in thy power? Why hast thou conceived this wickedness in thy heart? Thou hast not lied unto men but unto God." [1303] And below he says to the wife: "Why have ye agreed together to tempt the Spirit of the Lord?" [1304]

57. First, we understand that he called the Holy Spirit the Spirit of the Lord. Then, since he mentioned first the Holy Spirit and added: "Thou hast not lied unto men but unto God," you must

necessarily either understand the oneness of the Godhead in the Holy Spirit, since when the Holy Spirit is tempted a lie is told to God; or, if you endeavour to exclude the oneness of the Godhead, you yourself according to the words of Scripture certainly believe Him to be God.

58. For if we understand that these expressions are used both of the Spirit and of the Father, we certainly observe the unity of truth and knowledge in God the Father and the Holy Spirit, for falsehood is discovered alike by the Holy Spirit and by God the Father. But if we have received each truth concerning the Spirit, why do you, faithless man, attempt to deny what you read? Confess, then, either the oneness of the Godhead of the Father, of the Son, and of the Holy Spirit, or the Godhead of the Holy Spirit. Whichever you say, you will have said each in God, for both the Unity upholds the Godhead and the Godhead the Unity

[1298] Acts v. 9.

[1299] Rom. viii. 9.

[1300] Rom. viii. 10.

[1301] 2 Cor. xiii. 3.

[1302] 1 Cor. vii. 40.

[1303] Acts v. 3, 4.

[1304] Acts v. 5.

Chapter X.
The Divinity of the Holy Spirit is supported by a passage of St. John. This passage was, indeed, erased by heretics,

but it is a vain attempt, since their faithlessness could thereby more easily be convicted. The order of the context is considered in order that this passage may be shown to refer to the Spirit. He is born of the Spirit who is born again of the same Spirit, of Whom Christ Himself is believed to have been born and born again. Again, the Godhead of the Spirit is inferred from two testimonies of St. John; and lastly, it is explained how the Spirit, the water, and the blood are called witnesses.

59. Nor does the Scripture in this place alone bear witness to the theotes, that is, the Godhead of the Holy Spirit; but also the Lord Himself said in the Gospel: "The Spirit is God." [1305] Which passage you, Arians, so expressly testify to be said concerning the Spirit, that you remove it from your copies, [1306] and would that it were from yours and not also from those of the Church! For at the time when Auxentius [1307] had seized the Church of Milan with the arms and forces of impious unbelief, the Church of Sirmium [1308] was attacked by Valens and Ursatius, when their priests [i.e. bishops] failed in faith; this falsehood and sacrilege of yours was found in the ecclesiastical books. And it may chance that you did the same in the past.

60. And you have indeed been able to blot out the letters, but could not remove the faith. That erasure betrayed you more, that erasure condemned you more; and you were not able to obliterate the truth, but that erasure blotted out your names from the book of life. Why was the passage removed, "For God is a Spirit," if it did not pertain to the Spirit? For if you will have it that the expression is used of God the Father, you, who think it should be erased, deny, in consequence, God the Father. Choose which you will, in each the snare of your own

impiety will bind you if you confess yourselves to be heathen by denying either the Father or the Spirit to be God. Therefore your confession wherein you have blotted out the Word of God remains, while you fear the original.

61. You have blotted it out, indeed, in your breasts and minds, but the Word of God is not blotted out, the Holy Spirit is not blotted out, but turns away from impious minds; not grace but iniquity is blotted out; for it is written: "I am He, I am He that blot out thine iniquities." [1309] Lastly, Moses, making request for the people, says: "Blot me out of Thy book, if Thou sparest not this people." [1310] And yet he was not blotted out, because he had no iniquity, but grace flowed forth.

62. You are, then, convicted by your own confession that you cannot say it was done with wisdom but with cunning. For by cunning you know that you are convicted by the evidence of that passage, and that your arguments cannot apply against that testimony. For whence else could the meaning of that place be derived, since the whole tenour of the passage is concerning the Spirit?

63. Nicodemus enquires about regeneration, and the Lord replies: "Verily, verily, I say unto thee, except a man be born again by water and the Spirit, he cannot enter into the kingdom of God." [1311] And that He might show that there is one birth according to the flesh, and another according to the Spirit, He added: "That which is born of the flesh is flesh, because it is born of the flesh; and that which is born of the Spirit is Spirit, because the Spirit is God." [1312] Follow out the whole course of the passage, and you will find that God has shut out your impiety by the fulness of His statement: "Marvel not," says He, "that I said, Ye must be born again. The Spirit breatheth where

He listeth, and thou hearest His voice, but knowest not whence He cometh or whither He goeth, so is every one who is born of the Spirit." [1313]

64. Who is he who is born of the Spirit, and is made Spirit, but he who is renewed in the Spirit of his mind? [1314] This certainly is he who is regenerated by water and the Holy Spirit, since we receive the hope of eternal life through the laver of regeneration and renewing of the Holy Spirit. [1315] And elsewhere the Apostle Peter says: "Ye shall be baptized with the Holy Spirit." [1316] For who is he that is baptized with the Holy Spirit but he who is born again through water and the Holy Spirit? Therefore the Lord said of the Holy Spirit, Verily, verily, I say unto thee, except a man be born again by water and the Spirit, he cannot enter into the kingdom of God. And therefore He declared that we are born of Him in the latter case, through Whom He said that we were born in the former. This is the sentence of the Lord; I rest on what is written, not on argument.

65. I ask, however, why, if there be no doubt that we are born again by the Holy Spirit, there should be any doubt that we are born of the Holy Spirit, since the Lord Jesus Himself was both born and born again of the Holy Spirit. And if you confess that He was born of the Holy Spirit, because you are not able to deny it, but deny that He was born again, it is great folly to confess what is peculiar to God, and deny what is common to men. And therefore that is well said to you which was said to the Jews: "If I told you earthly things and ye believe not, how shall ye believe if I tell you heavenly things?" [1317]

66. And yet we find each passage so written in Greek, that He said not, through the Spirit, but of the Spirit. For it stands thus:

amen, amen, lego soi, ean me tis gennethe ex hudatos kai Pneumatos, that is, of water and the Spirit. Therefore, since one ought not to doubt that "that which is born of the Spirit" is written of the Holy Spirit; there is no doubt but that the Holy Spirit also is God, according to that which is written, "the Spirit is God."

67. But the same Evangelist, that he might make it plain that he wrote this concerning the Holy Spirit, says elsewhere: "Jesus Christ came by water and blood, not in the water only, but by water and blood. And the Spirit beareth witness, because the Spirit is truth; for there are three witnesses, the Spirit, the water, and the blood; and these three are one." [1318]

68. Hear how they are witnesses: The Spirit renews the mind, the water is serviceable for the laver, and the blood refers to the price. For the Spirit made us children by adoption, the water of the sacred Font washed us, the blood of the Lord redeemed us. So we obtain one invisible and one visible testimony in a spiritual sacrament, for "the Spirit Himself beareth witness to our spirit." [1319] Though the fulness of the sacrament be in each, yet there is a distinction of office; so where there is distinction of office, there certainly is not equality of witness.

[1305] S. John iii. 6. See below S: 63, n. 4.

[1306] "The charge is an admirable illustration of the groundlessness of such accusations of wilful corruption of Scripture. The words in question have no Greek authority at all, and are obviously a comment." Westcott on S. John v. 6.

[1307] Auxentius, a Cappadocian, was ordained priest a.d. 343 by Gregory, the violent opponent of St. Athanasius. After the synod of Milan a.d. 355, when the bishop of that see,

Dionysius, having refused to renounce Athanasius and the Nicene faith, was banished, Auxentius was forcibly intruded as bishop, and, in spite of the efforts of St. Hilary of Poitiers and other Catholics, maintained his position till his death in 374.

[1308] The reference must be to the synods of Sirmium. In one held a.d. 351, against Photinus, there was a great attempt to make the semi-Arians appear orthodox, and St. Hilary accepted, while St. Athanasius rejected, their formula. Another synod was held a.d. 357, when the aged Hosius was tormented into accepting a formula, called by St. Hilary the "Sirmian blasphemy." Another, no less injurious to the faith, was held in 358, by the desire of Constantius. During this time--but forgeries and the loss of some patristic writings make the history of the whole period somewhat uncertain--dates the weakness of Liberius, so that St. Ambrose may well speak of nutantibus sacerdotibus. See Hefele, Conc. Geschichte, I. on the Sirmian synods; Athanasius, Vol. IV. in this series, p. 464 ff.; Dict. Chr. Biog. III. 171, art. "Hosius;" Socrates, H. E., in this series, Vol. II. pp. 56, 57, 58.

[1309] Isa. xliii. 25.

[1310] Ex. xxxii. 32.

[1311] S. John iii. 5.

[1312] S. John iii. 6. This is the full reading of the passage according to St. Ambrose, referred to above in S: 59.

[1313] S. John iii. 7, 8.

[1314] Eph. iv. 23.

[1315] Tit. iii. 5.

[1316] Acts xi. 16.

[1317] S. John iii. 12.

[1318] 1 John v. 6, 7, 8.

[1319] Rom. viii. 16.

Chapter XI.
The objection has been made, that the words of St. John, "The Spirit is God," are to be referred to God the Father; since Christ afterwards declares that God is to be worshipped in Spirit and in truth. The answer is, first, that by the word Spirit is sometimes meant spiritual grace; next, it is shown that, if they insist that the Person of the Holy Spirit is signified by the words "in Spirit," and therefore deny that adoration is due to Him, the argument tells equally against the Son; and since numberless passages prove that He is to be worshipped, we understand from this that the same rule is to be laid down as regards the Spirit. Why are we commanded to fall down before His footstool? Because by this is signified the Lord's Body, and as the Spirit was the Maker of this, it follows that He is to be worshipped, and yet it does not accordingly follow that Mary is to be worshipped. Therefore the worship of the Spirit is not done away with, but His union with the Father is expressed, when it is said that the Father is to be worshipped in Spirit, and this point is supported by similar expressions.

69. But perhaps reference may be made to the fact that in a later passage of the same book, the Lord again said that God is Spirit, but spoke of God the Father. For you have this passage in the Gospel: "The hour now is, when the true worshippers

shall worship the Father in Spirit and truth, for such also doth the Father seek. God is Spirit, and they that worship Him must worship in Spirit and truth." [1320] By this passage you wish not only to deny the divinity of the Holy Spirit, but also, from God being worshipped in Spirit, deduce a subjection of the Spirit.

70. To which point I will briefly answer that Spirit is often put for the grace of the Spirit, as the Apostle also said: "For the Spirit Himself intercedeth for us with groanings which cannot be uttered;" [1321] that is, the grace of the Spirit, unless perchance you have been able to hear the groanings of the Holy Spirit. Therefore here too God is worshipped, not in the wickedness of the heart, but in the grace of the Spirit. "For into a malicious soul wisdom does not enter," [1322] because "no one can call Jesus Lord but in the Holy Spirit." [1323] And immediately he adds: "Now there are diversities of gifts." [1324]

71. Now this cannot pertain to the fulness, nor to the dividing of the Spirit; for neither does the mind of man grasp His fulness, nor is He divided into any portions of Himself; but He pours into [the soul] the gift of spiritual grace, in which God is worshipped as He is also worshipped in truth, for no one worships Him except he who drinks in the truth of His Godhead with pious affection. And he certainly does not apprehend Christ as it were personally, nor the Holy Spirit personally.

72. Or if you think that this is said as it were personally of Christ and of the Spirit, then God is worshipped in truth in like manner as He is worshipped in Spirit. There is therefore either a like subjection, which God forbid that you should believe,

and the Son is not worshipped; or, which is true, there is a like grace of Unity, and the Spirit is worshipped.

73. Let us then here draw our inferences and put an end to the impious questionings of the Arians. For if they say that the Spirit is therefore not to be worshipped because God is worshipped in Spirit, let them then say that the Truth is not to be worshipped, because God is worshipped in truth. For although there be many truths, since it is written: "Truths are minished from the sons of men;" [1325] yet they are given by the Divine Truth, which is Christ, Who says: "I am the Way, the Truth, and the Life." [1326] If therefore they understand the truth in this passage from custom, let them also understand the grace of the Spirit, and there is no stumbling; or if they receive Christ as the Truth, let them deny that He is to be worshipped.

74. But they are refuted by the acts of the pious, and by the course of the Scriptures. For Mary worshipped Christ, and therefore is appointed to be the messenger of the Resurrection to the apostles, [1327] loosening the hereditary bond, and the huge offence of womankind. For this the Lord wrought mystically, "that where sin had exceedingly abounded, grace might more exceedingly abound." [1328] And rightly is a woman appointed [as messenger] to men; that she who first had brought the message of sin to man should first bring the message of the grace of the Lord.

75. And the apostles worshipped; and therefore they who bore the testimony of the faith received authority as to the faith. And the angels worshipped, of whom it is written: "And let all His angels worship Him." [1329]

76. But they worship not only His Godhead but also His Footstool, as it is written: "And worship His footstool, for it is holy." [1330] Or if they deny that in Christ the mysteries also of His Incarnation are to be worshipped, in which we observe as it were certain express traces of His Godhead, and certain ways of the Heavenly Word; let them read that even the apostles worshipped Him when He rose again in the glory of His Flesh. [1331]

77. Therefore if it do not at all detract from Christ, that God is worshipped in Christ, for Christ too is worshipped; [1332] it certainly also detracts nothing from the Spirit that God is worshipped in the Spirit, for the Spirit also is worshipped, as the Apostle has said: "We serve the Spirit of God," [1333] for he who serves worships also, as it is said in an earlier passage: "Thou shalt worship the Lord thy God, and Him only shalt thou serve." [1334]

78. But lest any one should perchance seem to elude the instance we have adduced, let us consider in what manner that which the prophet says, "Worship His Footstool," appears to refer to the mystery of the divine Incarnation, for we must not estimate the footstool from the custom of men. For neither has God a body, neither is He other than beyond measure, that we should think a footstool was laid down as a support for His feet. And we read that nothing besides God is to be worshipped, for it is written: "Thou shalt worship the Lord thy God, and Him only shalt thou serve." How, then, should the prophet, brought up under the Law, and instructed in the Law, give a precept against the Law? The question, then, is not unimportant, and so let us more diligently consider what the footstool is. For we read elsewhere: "The heaven is My throne,

and the earth the footstool of My feet." [1335] But the earth is not to be worshipped by us, for it is a creature of God.

79. Let us, however, see whether the prophet does not say that that earth is to be worshipped which the Lord Jesus took upon Him in assuming flesh. And so, by footstool is understood earth, but by the earth the Flesh of Christ, which we this day also adore [1336] in the mysteries, and which the apostles, as we said above, adored in the Lord Jesus; for Christ is not divided but is one; nor, when He is adored as the Son of God, is He denied to have been born of the Virgin. Since, then, the mystery of the Incarnation is to be adored, and the Incarnation is the work of the Spirit, as it is written, "The Holy Spirit shall come upon thee, and the power of the Most High shall overshadow thee, and that Holy Thing Which shall be born of thee shall be called the Son of God," [1337] without doubt the Holy Spirit also is to be adored, since He Who according to the flesh was born of the Holy Spirit is adored.

80. And let no one divert this to the Virgin Mary; Mary was the temple of God, not the God of the temple. And therefore He alone is to be worshipped Who was working in His temple.

81. It makes, then, nothing against our argument that God is worshipped in Spirit, for the Spirit also is worshipped. Although if we consider the words themselves, what else ought we to understand in the Father, the Son, and the Holy Spirit, but the unity of the same power. For what is "must worship in Spirit and in truth"? If, however, you do not refer this to the grace of the Spirit, nor the true faith of conscience; but, as we said, personally (if indeed this word person is fit to express the Divine Majesty), you must take it of Christ and of the Spirit.

82. What means, then, the Father is worshipped in Christ, except that the Father is in Christ, and the Father speaks in Christ, and the Father abides in Christ. Not, indeed, as a body in a body, for God is not a body; nor as a confused mixture [confusus in confuso], but as the true in the true, God in God, Light in Light; as the eternal Father in the co-eternal Son. So not an ingrafting of a body is meant, but unity of power. Therefore, by unity of power, Christ is jointly worshipped in the Father when God the Father is worshipped in Christ. In like manner, then, by unity of the same power the Spirit is jointly worshipped in God, when God is worshipped in the Spirit.

83. Let us investigate the force of that word and expression more diligently, and deduce its proper meaning from other passages. "Thou hast," it is said, "made them all in wisdom." [1338] Do we here understand that Wisdom was without a share in the things that were made? But "all things were made by Him." [1339] And David says: "By the Word of the Lord were the heavens established." [1340] So, then, he himself who calls the Son of God the maker even of heavenly things, has also plainly said that all things were made in the Son, that in the renewal of His works He might by no means separate the Son from the Father, but unite Him to the Father.

84. Paul, too, says: "For in Him were all things created in the heavens and in the earth, visible and invisible." [1341] Does he, then, when he says, "in Him," deny that they were made through Him? Certainly he did not deny but affirmed it. And further he says in another place: "One Lord Jesus, through Whom are all things." [1342] In saying, then, "through Him," has he denied that all things were made in Him, through Whom he says that all things exist? These words, "in Him" and "with

Him," have this force, that by them is understood one and like in all respects, not contrary. Which he also made clear farther on, saying: "All things have been created through Him and in Him;" [1343] for, as we said above, Scripture witnesses that these three expressions, "with Him," and "through Him," and "in Him," are equivalent in Christ. [1344] For you read that all things were made through Him and in Him.

85. Learn also that the Father was with Him, and He with the Father, when all things were being made. Wisdom says: "When He was preparing the heavens I was with Him, when He was making the fountains of waters." [1345] And in the Old Testament the Father, by saying, "Let Us make," [1346] showed that the Son was to be worshipped with Himself as the Maker of all things. As, then, those things are said to have been created in the Son, of which the Son is received as the Creator; so, too, when God is said to be worshipped in truth by the proper meaning of the word itself often expressed after the same manner it ought to be understood, that the Son too is worshipped. So in like manner is the Spirit also worshipped because God is worshipped in Spirit. Therefore the Father is worshipped both with the Son and with the Spirit, because the Trinity is worshipped.

[1320] S. John iv. 23, 24.

[1321] Rom. viii. 26.

[1322] Wisd. i. 4.

[1323] 1 Cor. xii. 3.

[1324] 1 Cor. xii. 4.

[1325] Ps. xii. [xi.] 1.

[1326] S. John xiv. 6.

[1327] S. John xx. 17, 18.

[1328] Rom. v. 20.

[1329] Heb. i. 6.

[1330] Ps. xcix. [xcviii.] 5.

[1331] S. Matt. xxviii. 17.

[1332] St. Ambrose here argues against Apollinarianism, who separated the two natures in Christ and taught that He should not be adored except in His Godhead, giving to the orthodox the nickname of anthropolatrai. The Apollinarians held that Christ was Theos sarkophoros, as Nestorians made Him anthropos Theophoros, instead of the proper Theanthropos. Apollinaris said Christ is oute anthropos haplos, oute Theos, alla Theou kai anthropou mixis. He denied the complete human nature of our Lord, saying that the Logos supplied the place of the anima rationalis. This stunted humanity could not be accepted by the Church, as it would involve a merely partial redemption. Christ must be a perfect man, in order to be a perfect Redeemer. The heresy was opposed by St. Athanasius, St. Basil, and others, condemned in synods at Alexandria 362, Rome 373 and probably 382, Antioch 378 or 379, and decisively at Constantinople in the second oecumenical council. See Dict. Chr. Biog.; Blunt, Dict. of Sects, etc.; Hefele on Council of Constantinople; St. Gregory of Nazianzus' Letters on the Apollinarian controversy in this series, p. 437 ff.

[1333] Phil. iii. 3.

[1334] Deut. vi. 13.

[1335] Isa. lxvi. 1.

[1336] There can be no doubt that St. Ambrose held what is known as the Real Presence in the Sacrament of the Eucharist, and is here asserting the custom of his day, viz., that Christ was worshipped as indivisibly God and Man in that Sacrament. Similar expressions are to be found in other Fathers, and in St. Ambrose elsewhere; e.g. De Fide, V. 10; De Mysteriis, S:S: 52-54, 58. Bishop Andrewes, formerly of Winchester (ob. a.d. 1626), refers to St. Ambrose as follows: "Nos vero et in Mysteriis Carnem Christi adoramus cum Ambrosio, et non id, sed eum qui super altare colitur. Nec Carnem manducamus quin adoremus prius cum Augustino....El Sacramentum tamen nulli adoremus." Resp. ad Bellarmin, p. 195.

[1337] S. Luke i. 35.

[1338] Ps. civ. [ciii.] 24.

[1339] S. John i. 3.

[1340] Ps. xxxiii. [xxxii.] 6.

[1341] Col. i. 16.

[1342] 1 Cor. viii. 6.

[1343] Col. i. 16.

[1344] Bk. II. 8, 9.

[1345] Prov. viii. 27.

[1346] Gen. i. 26.

Chapter XII.

From the fact that St. Paul has shown that the light of the Godhead which the three apostles worshipped in Christ is in the Trinity, it is made clear that the Spirit also is to be worshipped. It is shown from the words themselves that the Spirit is intended by the apostles. The Godhead of the same Spirit is proved from the fact that He has a temple wherein He dwells not as a priest, but as God: and is worshipped with the Father and the Son; whence is understood the oneness of nature in Them.

86. But does any one deny that the Godhead of the eternal Trinity is to be worshipped? whereas the Scriptures also express the inexplicable Majesty of the Divine Trinity, as the Apostle says elsewhere: "Since God, Who said that light should shine out of darkness, shined in our hearts to give the light of the knowledge of the glory of God in the face of Jesus Christ." [1347]

87. The apostles truly saw this glory, when the Lord Jesus on the mount shone with the light of His Godhead: "The apostles," it says, "saw it and fell on their face." [1348] Do not you think that they even, as they fell, worshipped, when they could not with their bodily eyes endure the brightness of the divine splendour, and the glory of eternal light dulled the keenness of mortal sight? Or what else did they who saw His glory say at that time, except, "O come let us worship and fall down before Him"? [1349] For "God shined in our hearts to give the light of the knowledge of the glory of God in the face of Jesus Christ." [1350]

88. Who is He, then, Who shined that we might know God in the face of Jesus Christ? For he said, "God shined," that the

glory of God might be known in the face of Jesus Christ. Whom else do we think but the manifested Spirit? Or who else is there besides the Holy Spirit to Whom the power of the Godhead may be referred? For they who exclude the Spirit must necessarily bring in another, who may with the Father and the Son receive the glory of the Godhead.

89. Let us then go back to the same words: "It is God Who shined in our hearts to give the light of the knowledge of the glory of God in the face of Jesus Christ." You have Christ plainly set forth. For Whose glory is said to give light but that of the Spirit? So, then, he set forth God Himself, since he spoke of the glory of God; if of the Father, it remains that "He who said that light should shine out of darkness, and shine in our hearts," be understood to be the Holy Spirit, for we cannot venerate any other with the Father and the Son. If, then, you understand the Spirit, Him also has the Apostle called God; it is necessary, then, that you also confess the Godhead of the Spirit, who now deny it.

90. But how shamelessly do you deny this, since you have read that the Holy Spirit has a temple. For it is written: "Ye are the temple of God, and the Holy Spirit dwelleth in you." [1351] Now God has a temple, a creature has no true temple. But the Spirit, Who dwelleth in us, has a temple. For it is written: "Your members are temples of the Holy Spirit." [1352]

91. But He does not dwell in the temple as a priest, nor as a minister, but as God, since the Lord Jesus Himself said: "I will dwell in them, and will walk among them, and will be their God, and they shall be My people." [1353] And David says: "The Lord is in His holy temple." [1354] Therefore the Spirit dwells in His holy temple, as the Father dwells and as the Son

dwells, Who says: "I and the Father will come, and will make Our abode with him." [1355]

92. But the Father abides in us through the Spirit, Whom He has given us. How, then, can different natures abide together? Certainly it is impossible. But the Spirit abides with the Father and the Son. Whence, too, the Apostle joined the Communion of the Holy Spirit with the grace of Jesus Christ and the love of God, saying: "The grace of our Lord Jesus Christ, and the love of God, and the Communion of the Holy Spirit be with you all." [1356]

91. We observe, then, that the Father, the Son, and the Holy Spirit abide in one and the same [subject] through the oneness of the same nature. Therefore, He Who dwells in the temple has divine power, for as of the Father and of the Son, so are we also the temple of the Holy Spirit; not many temples, but one temple, for it is the temple of one Power.

[1347] 2 Cor. iv. 6.

[1348] S. Matt. xvii. 6.

[1349] Ps. xcv. [xciv.] 6.

[1350] 2 Cor. iv. 6.

[1351] 1 Cor. iii. 16.

[1352] 1 Cor. vi. 19.

[1353] Lev. xxvi. 12.

[1354] Ps. xi. [x.] 4.

[1355] S. John xiv. 23.

[1356] 2 Cor. xiii. 14.

Chapter XIII.
To those who object that Catholics, when they ascribe Godhead to the Holy Spirit, introduce three Gods, it is answered, that by the same argument they themselves bring in two Gods, unless they deny Godhead to the Son; after which the orthodox doctrine is set forth.

92. But what do you fear? Is it that which you have been accustomed to carp at? lest you should make three Gods. God forbid; for where the Godhead is understood as one, one God is spoken of. For neither when we call the Son God do we say there are two Gods. For if, when you confess the Godhead of the Spirit, you think that three Gods are spoken of, then, too, when you speak of the Godhead of the Son because you are not able to deny it, you bring in two Gods. For it is necessary according to your opinion, if you think that God is the name of one person, not of one nature, that you either say that there are two Gods, or deny that the Son is God.

93. But let us free you from the charge of ignorance, though we do not excuse you from fault. For according to our opinion, because there is one God, one Godhead and oneness of power is understood. For as we say that there is one God, confessing the Father, and not denying the Son under the true Name of the Godhead; so, too, we exclude not the Holy Spirit from the Unity of the Godhead, and do not assert but deny that there are three Gods, because it is not unity but a division of power which makes plurality. For how can the Unity of the Godhead admit of plurality, seeing that plurality is of numbers, but the Divine Nature does not admit numbers?

Chapter XIV.
Besides the evidence adduced above, other passages can
be brought to prove the sovereignty of the Three Persons.
Two are quoted from the Epistles to the Thessalonians,
and by collating other testimonies of the Scriptures it is
shown that in them dominion is claimed for the Spirit as
for the other Persons. Then, by quotation of another still
more express passage in the second Epistle to the
Corinthians, it is inferred both that the Spirit is Lord, and
that where the Lord is, there is the Spirit.

94. God, then, is One, without violation of the majesty of the
eternal Trinity, as is declared in the instance set before us. And
not in that place alone do we see the Trinity expressed in the
Name of the Godhead; but both in many places, as we have
said also above, and especially in the epistles which the Apostle
wrote to the Thessalonians, he most clearly set forth the
Godhead and sovereignty of the Father, the Son, and the Holy
Spirit. For you read as follows: "The Lord make you to increase
and abound in love one toward another, and toward all men, as
we also do toward you, to the stablishing of your hearts without
blame in holiness before God and our Father at the coming of
the Lord Jesus." [1357]

95. Who, then, is the Lord Who makes us to increase and
abound before God and our Father at the coming of the Lord
Jesus? He has named the Father and has named the Son;
Whom, then, has he joined with the Father and the Son except
the Spirit? Who is the Lord Who establishes our hearts in
holiness. For holiness is a grace of the Spirit, as, too, is said
farther on: "In holiness of the Spirit and belief of the truth."
[1358]

96. Who, then, do you think is here named Lord, except the Spirit? And has not God the Father been able to teach you, Who says: "Upon Whomsoever thou shalt see the Spirit descending and abiding upon Him, this is He Who baptizeth in the Holy Spirit"? [1359] For the Spirit descended in the likeness of a dove, [1360] that He might both bear witness to His wisdom, and perfect the sacrament of the spiritual laver, and show that His working is one with that of the Father and the Son.

97. And that you should not suppose that anything had fallen from the Apostle by oversight, but that he knowingly and designedly and inspired by the Spirit designated Him Lord, Whom he felt to be God, he repeated the same in the second Epistle to the Thessalonians, saying: "But the Lord direct your hearts in the love of God and in the patience of Christ." [1361] If love be of God and patience of Christ, it ought to be shown Who is the Lord Who directs, if we deny that the direction is of the Holy Spirit.

98. But we cannot deny it, since the Lord said of Him: "I have yet many things to say unto you, but ye cannot bear them now. But when He, the Spirit of Truth, shall come, He will lead you into all truth." [1362] And David says of Him: "Thy good Spirit shall lead me into the right way." [1363]

99. See what the voice of the Lord uttered concerning the Holy Spirit. The Son of God came, and because He had not yet shed forth the Spirit, He declared that we were living like little children without the Spirit. He said that the Spirit was to come Who should make of these little children stronger men, by an increase, namely, of spiritual age. And this He laid down not that He might set the power of the Spirit in the first place, but

211

that He might show that the fulness of strength consists in the knowledge of the Trinity.

100. It is therefore necessary either that you mention some fourth person besides the Spirit of whom you ought to be conscious, or assuredly that you do not consider another to be Lord, except the Spirit Who has been pointed out.

101. But if you require the plain statement of the words in which Scripture has spoken of the Spirit as Lord, it cannot have escaped you that it is written: "Now the Lord is the Spirit." [1364] Which the course of the whole passage shows to have been certainly said of the Holy Spirit. And so let us consider the apostolic statement: "As often as Moses is read," says he, "a veil is laid over their heart; but when they shall be turned to the Lord, the veil shall be taken away. Now the Lord is the Spirit; but where the Spirit of the Lord is, there is liberty." [1365]

102. So he not only called the Spirit Lord, but also added: "But where the Spirit of the Lord is, there is liberty. So we all with unveiled face, reflecting the glory of the Lord, are formed anew into the same image from glory to glory, as from the Lord the Spirit;" [1366] that is, we who have been before converted to the Lord, so as by spiritual understanding to see the glory of the Lord, as it were, in the mirror of the Scriptures, are now being transformed from that glory which converted us to the Lord, to the heavenly glory. Therefore since it is the Lord to Whom we are converted, but the Lord is that Spirit by Whom we are formed anew, who are converted to the Lord, assuredly the Holy Ghost is pointed out, for He Who forms anew receives those who are converted. For how should He form again those whom He had not received.

103. Though why should we seek for the expression of words, where we see the expression of unity? For although you may distinguish between Lord and Spirit, you cannot deny that where the Lord is, there too is the Spirit, and he who has been converted to the Lord will have been converted to the Spirit. If you cavil at the letter, you cannot injure the Unity; if you wish to separate the Unity, you confess the Spirit Himself as the Lord of power.

[1357] 1 Thess. iii. 12, 13.

[1358] 2 Thess. ii. 13.

[1359] S. John i. 33.

[1360] S. Luke iii. 22.

[1361] 2 Thess. iii. 5.

[1362] S. John xvi. 12, 13.

[1363] Ps. cxliii. [cxlii.] 10.

[1364] 2 Cor. iii. 17.

[1365] 2 Cor. iii. 15-17.

[1366] 2 Cor. iii. 17, 18.

Chapter XV.

Though the Spirit be called Lord, three Lords are not thereby implied; inasmuch as two Lords are not implied by the fact that the Son in the same manner as the Father is called Lord in many passages of Scripture; for Lordship exists in the Godhead, and the Godhead in Lordship, and these coincide without division in the Three Persons.

104. But perhaps, again, you may say: If I call the Spirit Lord, I shall set forth three Lords. Do you then when you call the Son Lord either deny the Son or confess two Lords? God forbid, for the Son Himself said: "Do not serve two lords." [1367] But certainly He denied not either Himself or the Father to be Lord; for He called the Father Lord, as you read: "I thank Thee, O Father, Lord of heaven and earth." [1368] And the Lord spoke of Himself, as we read in the Gospel: "Ye call Me Master and Lord, and ye do well, for so I am." [1369] But He spoke not of two Lords; indeed He shows that He did not speak of two Lords, when He warns them: "Do not serve two lords." For there are not two Lords where the Lordship is but one, for the Father is in the Son and the Son in the Father, and so there is one Lord.

105. Such, too, was the teaching of the Law: "Hear, O Israel, the Lord thy God is one Lord," [1370] that is, unchangeable, always abiding in unity of power, always the same, and not altered by any accession or diminution. Therefore Moses called Him One, and yet also relates that the Lord rained down fire from the Lord. [1371] The Apostle, too, says: "The Lord grant unto him to find mercy of the Lord." [1372] The Lord rains down from the Lord; the Lord grants mercy from the Lord. The Lord is neither divided when He rains from the Lord, nor

is there a separation when He grants mercy from the Lord, but in each case the oneness of the Lordship is expressed.

106. In the Psalms, too, you find: "The Lord said unto my Lord." [1373] And he did not therefore deny that the Father was his Lord, because he spoke of the Son as his Lord; but therefore called the Son his Lord, that you might not think Him to be the Son, but the Lord of the prophet, as the Lord Himself showed in the Gospel, when He said: "If David in the Spirit called Him Lord, how is he his Son?" [1374] David, not the Spirit, calls Him Lord in the Spirit. Or if they falsely infer from this that the Spirit called Him Lord, they must necessarily by a like sacrilege seem to assert that the Son of God is also the Son of the Spirit.

107. So, as we do not say that there are two Lords, when we so style both the Father and the Son, so, too, we do not say that there are three Lords, when we confess the Spirit to be Lord. For as it is profane to say that there are three Lords or three Gods, so, too, is it utter profanity to speak of two Lords or two Gods; for there is one God, one Lord, one Holy Spirit; and He Who is God is Lord, and He Who is Lord is God, for the Godhead is in the Lordship, and the Lordship is in the Godhead.

108. Lastly, you have read that the Father is both Lord and God: "O Lord my God, I will call upon Thee, hear Thou me." [1375] You find the Son to be both Lord and God, as you have read in the Gospel, that, when Thomas had touched the side of Christ, he said, "My Lord and my God." [1376] So in like manner as the Father is God and the Son Lord, so too the Son is God and the Father Lord. The holy designation changes from one to the other, the divine nature changes not, but the

dignity remains unchangeable. For they are not [as it were] contributions gathered from bounty, but free-will gifts of natural love; for both Unity has its special property, and the special properties are bound together in unity.

[1367] S. Matt. vi. 24.

[1368] S. Matt. xi. 25.

[1369] S. John xiii. 13.

[1370] Deut. vi. 4.

[1371] Gen. xix. 24.

[1372] 2 Tim. i. 18.

[1373] Ps. cx. [cix.] 1.

[1374] S. Matt. xxii. 43, 45.

[1375] Ps. xxx. [xxix.] 2.

[1376] S. John xx. 28.

Chapter XVI.
The Father is holy, and likewise the Son and the Spirit, and so They are honoured in the same Trisagion: nor can we speak more worthily of God than by calling Him Holy; whence it is clear that we must not derogate from the dignity of the Holy Spirit. In Him is all which pertains to God, since in baptism He is named with the Father and the Son, and the Father has given to Him to be greater than all, nor can any one deprive Him of this. And so from the very passage of St. John which heretics used against His dignity, the equality of the Trinity and the Unity of

the Godhead is established. Lastly, after explaining how the Son receives from the Father, St. Ambrose shows how various heresies are refuted by the passage cited.

109. So, then, the Father is holy, the Son is holy, and the Spirit is holy, but they are not three Holies; [1377] for there is one Holy God, one Lord. For the true holiness is one, as the true Godhead is one, as that true holiness belonging to the Divine Nature is one.

110. So everything which we esteem holy proclaims that Sole Holiness. Cherubim and Seraphim with unwearied voices praise Him and say: "Holy, Holy, Holy, is the Lord God of Sabaoth." [1378] They say it, not once, lest you should believe that there is but one; not twice, lest you should exclude the Spirit; they say not holies [in the plural], lest you should imagine that there is plurality, but they repeat thrice and say the same word, that even in a hymn you may understand the distinction of Persons in the Trinity, and the oneness of the Godhead and while they say this they proclaim God.

111. We too find nothing of more worth, whereby we are able to proclaim God, than the calling Him holy. Everything is too low for God, too low for the Lord. And therefore consider from this fact also whether one ought at all to derogate from the Holy Spirit, whose Name is the praise of God. For thus is the Father praised, thus is the Son also praised, in the same manner as the Spirit also is named and praised. The Seraphim utter praise, the whole company of the blessed utter praise, inasmuch as they call God holy, the Son holy, the Spirit holy.

112. How, then, does He not possess all that pertains to God, Who is named by priests in baptism with the Father and the Son, and is invoked in the oblations, is proclaimed by the

Seraphim in heaven with the Father and the Son, dwells in the Saints with the Father and the Son, is poured upon the just, is given as the source of inspiration to the prophets? And for this reason in the divine Scripture all is called theopneustos, because God inspires what the Spirit has spoken.

113. Or if they are unwilling to allow that the Holy Spirit has all things which pertain to God, and can do all things, let them say what He has not, and what He cannot do. For like as the Son has all things, and the Father grudges not to give all things to the Son according to His nature, having given to Him that which is greater than all, as the Scripture bears witness, saying: "That which My Father hath given unto Me is greater than all." [1379] So too the Spirit has of Christ that which is greater than all, because righteousness knows not grudging.

114. So, then, if we attend diligently, we comprehend here also the oneness of the Divine Power. He says: "That which My Father hath given unto Me is greater than all, and no one is able to snatch them out of My Father's hand. I and the Father are One." [1380] For if we rightly showed above that the Holy Spirit is the Hand of the Father, the same is certainly the Hand of the Father which is the Hand of the Son, since the Same is the Spirit of the Father Who is the Spirit of the Son. Therefore whosoever of us receives eternal life in this Name of the Trinity, as he is not torn from the Father; so he is not torn from the Son, so too he is not torn from the Spirit.

115. Again, from the very fact that the Father is said to have given to the Son, and the Spirit to have received from the Son, as it is written: "He shall glorify Me, for He shall take of Mine, and shall declare it unto you" [1381] (which He seems to have said rather of the office of distributing, than of the prerogative

of Divine Power, for those whom the Son redeemed the Spirit also, Who was to sanctify them, received), from those very words, I say, from which they construct their sophistry, the Unity of the Godhead is perceived, not the need of a gift.

116. The Father gave by begetting, not by adoption; He gave as it were that which was contained in the very prerogative of the Divine Nature, not what was lacking as it were by favour of His bounty. And so because the Son acquires persons to Himself as the Father does; so gives life as does the Father, He expressed His equality with the Father in the Unity of Power, saying: "I and the Father are One." For when He says, "I and the Father," equality is revealed; when He says, "are One," Unity is asserted. Equality excludes confusion; Unity excludes separation. Equality distinguishes between the Father and the Son; Unity does not separate the Father and the Son.

117. Therefore, when He says, "I and the Father," He rejects the Sabellian, for He says that He is one, the Father another; He rejects the Photinian, for He joins Himself with God the Father. With the former words He rejects those, for He said: "I and the Father;" with the latter words He rejects the Arians, for He says: "are One." Yet in both the former and the latter words He refutes the heretical violence (1) of the Sabellians, for He said: "We are One [Substance]," not "We are One[Person]." And (2) of the Arians, for He said: "I and the Father," not "the Father and I." Which was certainly not a sign of rudeness, but of dutifulness and foreknowledge, that we might not think wrongly from the order of the words. For unity knows no order, equality knows no gradation; nor can it be laid to the Son of God that the Teacher Himself of dutifulness should offend against dutifulness by rudeness.

[1377] This is, of course, to be understood as in the Athanasian Creed. The attributes of eternity, omnipotence, etc., are ascribed to each of the Three Persons, and we are then told that there are not three Eternals, etc. Each Person of the Holy Trinity possesses each attribute, but the attributes are all one and cannot be divided any more than the Godhead. Each Person is holy, but there are not, so to say, three separate Holinesses.

[1378] Isa. vi. 3.

[1379] S. John x. 29.

[1380] S. John x. 29, 30.

[1381] S. John xvi. 14.

Chapter XVII.
St. Ambrose shows by instances that the places in which those words were spoken help to the understanding of the words of the Lord; he shows that Christ uttered the passage quoted from St. John in Solomon's porch, by which is signified the mind of a wise man, for he says that Christ would not have uttered this saying in the heart of a foolish or contentious man. He goes on to say that Christ is stoned by those who believe not these words, and as the keys of heaven were given to Peter for his confession of them, so Iscariot, because he believed not the same, perished evilly. He takes this opportunity to inveigh against the Jews who bought the Son of God and sold Joseph. He explains the price paid for each mystically; and having in the same manner expounded the murmuring of the traitor concerning Magdalene's ointment, he adds that Christ is bought in one way by

heretics in another way by Catholics, and that those in vain take to themselves the name of Christians who sever the Spirit from the Father.

118. It is worth while to notice in what place the Lord held this discussion, for His utterances are often [better] estimated by the kind of places in which He conversed. When about to fast, He is led (as we read) into the wilderness to render vain the devil's temptations. For although it deserves praise to have lived temperately in the midst of abundance, yet the enticements of temptation are more frequent amongst riches and pleasures. Then the tempter, in order to try Him, promises Him abundance, and the Lord in order to overcome cherishes hunger. Now I do not deny that temperance can exist in the midst of riches; but although he who navigates the sea often escapes, yet he is more exposed to peril than he who will not go to sea.

119. Let us consider some other points. When about to promise the kingdom of heaven, Jesus went up into a mountain. At another time He leads His disciples through the corn-fields, when about to sow in their minds the crop of heavenly precepts, so that a plentiful harvest of souls should ripen. When about to consummate the work of the flesh which He had taken, having now seen perfection in His disciples, whom He had established upon the root of His words, He enters a garden, that He might plant the young olive-trees [1382] in the house of the Lord, and that He might water the just flourishing like a palm-tree, [1383] and the fruitful vine with the stream of His Blood.

120. In this passage too He was walking, as we read, in Solomon's porch on the day of the dedication, that is, Christ

was walking in the breast of the wise and prudent, to dedicate his good affection to Himself. What that porch was the prophet teaches, saying: "I will walk in the midst of Thy house in the innocency of my heart." [1384] So, then, we have in our own selves the house of God, we have the halls, we have also the porches, and we have the courts, for it is written: "Let thy waters flow abroad in thy courts." [1385] Open, then, this porch of thy heart to the Word of God, Who says to thee: "Open thy mouth wide and I will fill it." [1386]

121. Let us, therefore, hear what the Word of God, walking in the heart of the wise and peaceful, says: "I and My Father are One." [1387] He will not say this in the breast of the unquiet and foolish, for "the natural man receiveth not the things of the Spirit of God, for they are foolishness unto him." [1388] The narrow breasts of sinners do not take in the greatness of the faith. Lastly, the Jews hearing, "I and the Father are One, took up stones to stone Him." [1389]

122. He who cannot listen to this is a Jew; he who cannot listen to this stones Christ with the stones of his treachery, rougher than any rock, and if you believe me, he wounds Christ. For although He cannot now feel a wound: "For now henceforth we know not Christ after the flesh," [1390] yet He Who rejoices in the love of the Church is stoned by the impiety of the Arians.

123. "The law of Thy mouth, O Lord, is good unto me, I keep Thy commandments." [1391] Thou hast Thyself said that Thou art one with the Father. Because Peter believed this, he received the keys of the kingdom of heaven, and without anxiety for himself forgave sins. Judas, because he believed not this, strangled himself with the cord of his own wickedness. O the

hard stones of unbelieving words! O the unseemly cord of the betrayer, and the still more hideous purchase-money of the Jews! O hateful money wherewith either the just is bought for death, or sold! Joseph was sold, Jesus Christ was bought, the one to slavery, the Other to death. O detestable inheritance, O deadly sale, which either sells a brother to suffering or sets a price on the Lord to destroy Him, the Purchaser of the salvation of all.

124. The Jews did violence to two things which are chief of all, faith and duty, and in each to Christ the Author of faith and duty. For both in the patriarch Joseph was there a type of Christ, and Christ Himself came in the truth of His Body, "Who counted it not robbery that He should be equal with God, but took on Him the form of a servant," [1392] because of our fall, that is to say, taking slavery upon Himself and not shrinking from suffering.

125. In one place the sale is for twenty pieces, in the other for thirty. For how could His true price be apprehended, Whose value cannot be limited? There is error in the price because there is error in the inquiry. The sale is for twenty pieces in the Old Testament, for thirty in the New; for the Truth is of more value than the type, Grace is more generous than training, the Presence is better than the Law, for the Law promised the Coming, the Coming fulfilled the Law.

126. The Ishmaelites made their purchase for twenty pieces, the Jews for thirty. And this is no trivial figure. The faithless are more lavish for iniquity than the faithful for salvation. It is, however, fitting to consider the quality of each agreement. Twenty pieces are the price of him sold to slavery, thirty pieces of Him delivered to the Cross. For although the Mysteries of

the Incarnation and of the Passion must be in like manner matters of amazement, yet the fulfilment of faith is in the Mystery of the Passion. I do not indeed value less the birth from the holy Virgin, but I receive even more gratefully the Mystery of the sacred Body. What is more full of mercy than that He should forgive me the wrongs done to Himself? But it is even fuller measure that He gave us so great a gift, that He Who was not to die because He was God, should die by our death, that we might live by His Spirit.

127. Lastly, it was not without meaning that Judas Iscariot valued that ointment at three hundred pence, which seems certainly by the statement of the price itself to set forth the Lord's cross. Whence, too, the Lord says: "For she, pouring this ointment on My body, did it for My burial." [1393] Why, then, did Judas value this at so high a rate? Because remission of sins is of more value to sinners, and forgiveness seems to be more precious. Lastly, you find it written: "To whom much is forgiven the same loveth more." [1394] Therefore sinners themselves also confess the grace of the Lord's Passion which they have lost, and they bear witness to Christ who persecuted Him.

128. Or because, "into a malicious soul wisdom does not enter," [1395] the evil disposition of the traitor uttered this, and he valued the suffering of the Lord's body at a dearer rate, that by the immensity of the price he might draw all away from the faith. And therefore the Lord offered Himself without price, that the necessity of poverty might hold no one back from Christ. The patriarchs sold Him for a small price that all might buy. Isaiah said: "Ye that have no money go buy and drink; eat ye without money," [1396] that he might gain him who had no money. O traitor Judas, thou valuest the ointment of His

Passion at three hundred pence, and sellest His Passion for thirty pence. [1397] Profuse in valuing, mean in selling.

129. So, then, all do not buy Christ at the same price; Photinus, who buys Him for death, buys Him at one price; the Arian, who buys Him to wrong Him, at another price; the Catholic, who buys Him to glorify Him, at another. But he buys Him without money according to that which is written: "He that hath no money let him buy without price." [1398]

130. "Not all," says Christ, "that say unto Me, Lord, Lord, shall enter into the kingdom of heaven!" [1399] Although many call themselves Christians, and make use of the name, yet not all shall receive the reward. Both Cain offered sacrifice, and Judas received the kiss, but it was said to him, "Judas, betrayest thou the Son of Man with a kiss?" [1400] that is, thou fillest up thy wickedness with the pledge of affection, and sowest hatred with the implement of peace, and inflictest death with the outward token of love.

131. Let not, then, the Arians flatter themselves with the employment of the name, because they call themselves Christians. The Lord will answer them: You set forward My Name, and deny My Substance, but I do not recognize My Name where My eternal Godhead is not. That is not My Name which is divided from the Father, and separated from the Spirit; I do not recognize My Name where I do not recognize My doctrine; I do not recognize My Name where I do not recognize My Spirit. For he knows not that he is comparing the Spirit of the Father to those servants whom He created. Concerning which point we have already spoken at length. [1401]

[1382] Ps. cxxviii. [cxxvii.] 3.

[1383] Ps. xcii. [xci.] 12.

[1384] Ps. ci. [c.] 2.

[1385] Prov. v. 16.

[1386] Ps. lxxxi. [lxxx.] 10.

[1387] S. John x. 30.

[1388] 2 Cor. ii. 14.

[1389] S. John x. 31.

[1390] 2 Cor. v. 16.

[1391] Ps. cxix. [cxviii.] 72, 73.

[1392] Phil. ii. 6, 7.

[1393] S. Matt. xxvi. 12.

[1394] S. Luke vii. 47.

[1395] Wisd. i. 4.

[1396] Isa. lv. 1.

[1397] St. Ambrose is not quite accurate here in his proportions, though the point is in itself immaterial. The denarius, or "penny," was worth about ninepence, and was the day wage of a labourer; the shekel or "piece of silver," was worth more, being of the value of four denarii. Thirty shekels was the price of a slave.

[1398] Isa. lv. 1, 2.

[1399] S. Matt. vii. 21.

[1400] S. Luke xxii. 48.

[1401] Book I. 1.

Chapter XVIII.

As he purposes to establish the Godhead of the Holy Spirit by the points already discussed, St. Ambrose touches again on some of them; for instance, that He does not commit but forgives sin; that He is not a creature but the Creator; and lastly, that He does not offer but receives worship.

132. But to sum up, in order at the end more distinctly to gather up the arguments which have been used here and there, the evident glory of the Godhead is proved both by other arguments, and most especially by these four. God is known by these marks: either that He is without sin; or that He forgives sin; or that He is not a creature but the Creator; or that He does not give but receives worship.

133. So, then, no one is without sin except God alone, for no one is without sin except God. [1402] Also, no one forgives sins except God alone, for it is also written: "Who can forgive sins but God alone?" [1403] And one cannot be the Creator of all except he be not a creature, and he who is not a creature is without doubt God; for it is written: "They worshipped the creature rather than the Creator, Who is God blessed for ever." [1404] God also does not worship, but is worshipped, for it is written: "Thou shalt worship the Lord thy God, and Him only shalt thou serve." [1405]

134. Let us therefore consider whether the Holy Spirit have any of these marks which may bear witness to His Godhead. And first let us treat of the point that none is without sin except

God alone, and demand that they prove that the Holy Spirit has sin.

135. But they are unable to show us this, and demand our authority from us, namely, that we should show by texts that the Holy Spirit has not sinned, as it is said of the Son that He did no sin. [1406] Let them learn that we teach by authority of the Scriptures; for it is written: "For in Wisdom is a Spirit of understanding, holy, one only, manifold, subtle, easy to move, eloquent, undefiled." [1407] The Scripture says He is undefiled, has it lied concerning the Son, that you should believe it to have lied concerning the Spirit? For the prophet said in the same place concerning Wisdom, that nothing that defiles enters into her. She herself is undefiled, and her Spirit is undefiled. Therefore if the Spirit have not sin, He is God.

136. But how can He be guilty of sin Who Himself forgives sins? Therefore He has not committed sin, and if He be without sin He is not a creature. For every creature is exposed to the capability of sin, and the eternal Godhead alone is free from sin and undefiled.

137. Let us now see whether the Spirit forgives sins. But on this point there can be no doubt, since the Lord Himself said: "Receive ye the Holy Spirit. Whosoever sins ye forgive they shall be forgiven." [1408] See that sins are forgiven through the Holy Spirit. But men make use of their ministry for the forgiveness of sins, they do not exercise the right of any power of their own. For they forgive sins not in their own name but in that of the Father and of the Son and of the Holy Spirit. They ask, the Godhead gives, the service is of man, the gift is of the Power on high.

138. And it is not doubtful that sin is forgiven by means of baptism, but in baptism the operation is that of the Father and of the Son and of the Holy Spirit. If, therefore, the Spirit forgives sin, since it is written, "Who can forgive sins except God alone?" [1409] certainly He Who cannot be separated from the oneness of the name of the Nature is also incapable of being severed from the power of God. Now if He is not severed from the power of God, how is He severed from the name of God.

139. Let us now see whether He be a creature or the Creator. But since we have above [1410] most clearly proved Him to be the Creator, as it is written: "The Spirit of God Who hath made me;" [1411] and it has been declared that the face of the earth is renewed by the Spirit, and that all things languish without the Spirit, [1412] it is clear that the Spirit is the Creator. But who can doubt this, since, as we have shown above, not even the generation of the Lord from the Virgin, which is more excellent than all creatures, is without the operation of the Spirit?

140. Therefore the Spirit is not a creature, but the Creator, and He Who is Creator is certainly not a creature. And because He is not a creature, without doubt He is the Creator Who produces all things together with the Father and the Son. But if He be the Creator, certainly the Apostle, by saying in condemnation of the Gentiles, "Who served the creature rather than the Creator, Who is God blessed for ever," [1413] and by warning men, as I said above, that the Holy Spirit is to be served, both showed Him to be the Creator, and because He is the Creator demonstrated that He ought to be called God. Which he also sums up in the Epistle written to the Hebrews, saying: "For He that created all things is God." [1414] Let them, therefore, either say what it is which has been created

without the Father, Son, and Holy Spirit, or let them confess that the Spirit also is of one Godhead with the Father and the Son.

141. The writer taught also that He was to be worshipped, Whom he called Lord and God. For He Who is the God and Lord of the Universe is certainly to be worshipped by all, for it is thus written: "Thou shalt worship the Lord thy God, and Him only shalt thou serve." [1415]

142. Or let them say where they have read that the Spirit worships. For it is said of the Son of God: "Let all the Angels of God worship Him;" [1416] we do not read, Let the Spirit worship Him. For how can He worship Who is not amongst servants and ministers, but, together with the Father and the Son, has the service of the just under Him, for it is written: "We serve the Spirit of God." [1417] He is, therefore, to be worshipped by us, Whom the Apostle taught that we must serve, and Whom we serve we also adore, according to that which is written, to repeat the same words again: "Thou shalt worship the Lord thy God, and Him only shalt thou serve."

143. Although the Apostle has not omitted even this point, so as to omit to teach us that the Spirit is to be worshipped. For since we have demonstrated that the Spirit is in the prophets, no one can doubt that prophecy is given by the Spirit, and plainly when He Who is in the prophets is worshipped, the same Spirit is worshipped. And so you find: "If the whole Church be assembled together, and all speak with tongues, and there come in one unlearned or unbelieving, will he not say that ye are mad? But if all prophesy, and there come in one unlearned and unbelieving, he is convicted by all, he is judged by all. For the secrets of his heart are made manifest, and so

falling down on his face he will worship God, declaring that God is in truth among you." [1418] It is, therefore, God Who is worshipped, God Who abides and Who speaks in the prophets; but the Spirit thus abides and speaks, therefore, also, the Spirit is worshipped.

[1402] S. Matt. xix. 17.

[1403] S. Luke v. 21.

[1404] Rom. i. 25.

[1405] Deut. vi. 13.

[1406] 1 Pet. ii. 22.

[1407] Wisd. vii. 22.

[1408] S. John xx. 22.

[1409] S. Mark ii. 7.

[1410] Cp. B. II. 5, 6.

[1411] Job xxxiii. 4.

[1412] Ps. civ. [ciii.] 29, 30.

[1413] Rom. i. 25.

[1414] Heb. iii. 4.

[1415] Deut. vi. 13.

[1416] Heb. i. 6.

[1417] Phil. iii. 3.

[1418] 1 Cor. xiv. 23-25.

Chapter XIX.

Having proved above that the Spirit abides and speaks in the prophets, St. Ambrose infers that He knows all things which are of God, and therefore is One with the Father and the Son. This same point he establishes again from the fact that He possesses all that God possesses, namely, Godhead, knowledge of the heart, truth, a Name above every name, and power to raise the dead, as is proved from Ezekiel, and in this He is equal to the Son.

144. And so as the Father and the Son are One, because the Son has all things which the Father has, so too the Spirit is one with the Father and the Son, because He too knows all the things of God. For He did not obtain it by force, so that there should be any injury as of one who had suffered loss; He did not seize it, lest the loss should be his from whom it might seem to have been plundered. For neither did He seize it through need, nor through superiority of greater power did He take it by force, but He possesses it by unity of power. Therefore, if He works all these things, for one and the same Spirit worketh all, [1419] how is He not God Who has all things which God has?

145. Or let us consider what God may have which the Holy Spirit has not. God the Father has Godhead, and the Son, too, in Whom dwells the fulness of the Godhead, has it, and the Spirit has it, for it is written: "The Spirit of God is in my nostrils." [1420]

146. God, again, searches the hearts and reins, for it is written: "God searcheth the hearts and reins." [1421] The Son also has this power, Who said, "Why think ye evil in your hearts?"

[1422] For Jesus knew their thoughts. And the Spirit has the same power, Who manifests to the prophets also the secrets of the hearts of others, as we said above: "for the secrets of his heart are made manifest." And why do we wonder if He searches the hidden things of man Who searches even the deep things of God?

147. God has as an attribute that He is true for it is written: "Let God be true and every man a liar." [1423] Does the Spirit lie Who is the Spirit of Truth? [1424] and Whom we have shown to be called the Truth, since John called Him too the Truth, as also the Son? And David says in the psalm: "Send out Thy light and Thy truth, they have led me and brought me to Thy holy hill and to Thy tabernacles." [1425] If you consider that in this passage the Son is the light, then the Spirit is the Truth, or if you consider the Son to be the Truth, then the Spirit is the light.

148. God has a Name which is above every name, and has given a name to the Son, as we read that in the Name of Jesus knees should bow. Let us consider whether the Spirit has this Name. But it is written "Go, baptize the nations in the Name of the Father, and of the Son, and of the Holy Spirit." [1426] He has, then, a Name above every name. What, therefore, the Father and the Son have, the Holy Spirit also has through the oneness of the Name of His nature.

149. It is a prerogative of God to raise the dead. "For as the Father raiseth the dead and quickeneth them, so the Son also quickeneth whom He will." [1427] But the Spirit also (by Whom God raiseth) raiseth them, for it is written: "He shall quicken also your mortal bodies through His Spirit that dwelleth in you." [1428] But that you may not think this a trivial

grace, learn that the Spirit also raises, for the prophet Ezekiel says: "Come, O Spirit, and breathe upon these dead, and they shall live. And I prophesied as He commanded me, and the Spirit of life entered into them, and they lived, and stood up on their feet an exceeding great company." [1429] And farther on God says: "Ye shall know that I am the Lord, when I shall open your graves, that I may bring My people out of their graves, and I will give you My Spirit, and ye shall live." [1430]

150. When He spoke of His Spirit, did He mention any other besides the Holy Spirit? For He would neither have spoken of His Spirit as produced by blowing, nor could this Spirit come from the four quarters of the world, for the blowing of these winds, which we experience, is partial, not universal; and this spirit by which we live is also individual, not universal. But it is the nature of the Holy Spirit to be both over all and in all. Therefore from the words of the prophet we may see how (the frame-work of the members long since fallen asunder being scattered) the bones may come together again to the form of a revived body, when the Spirit quickens them; and the ashes may come together on the limbs belonging to them, animated by a disposition to come together before being formed anew in the appearance of living.

151. Do we not in the likeness of what is done recognize the oneness of the divine power? The Spirit raises after the same manner as the Lord raised at the time of His own Passion, when suddenly in the twinkling of an eye the graves of the dead were opened, and the bodies living again arose from the tombs, and the smell of death being removed, and the scent of life restored, the ashes of those who were dead took again the likeness of the living.

152. So, then, the Spirit has that which Christ has, and therefore what God has, for all things which the Father has the Son also has, and therefore He said: "All things which the Father hath are Mine." [1431]

[1419] 1 Cor. xii. 11.

[1420] Job xxvii. 3.

[1421] Ps. vii. 9.

[1422] S. Matt. ix. 4.

[1423] Rom. iii. 4.

[1424] S. John xvi. 13.

[1425] Ps. xliii. [xlii.] 3.

[1426] S. Matt. xxviii. 19.

[1427] S. John v. 21.

[1428] Rom. viii. 11.

[1429] Ezek. xxxvii. 9, 10.

[1430] Ezek. xxxvii. 13, 14.

[1431] S. John xvi. 15.

Chapter XX.

The river flowing from the Throne of God is a figure of the Holy Spirit, but by the waters spoken of by David the powers of heaven are intended. The kingdom of God is the work of the Spirit; and it is no matter for wonder if He

reigns in this together with the Son, since St. Paul promises that we too shall reign with the Son.

153. And this, again, is not a trivial matter that we read that a river goes forth from the throne of God. For you read the words of the Evangelist John to this purport: "And He showed me a river of living water, bright as crystal, proceeding out of the throne of God and of the Lamb. In the midst of the street thereof, and on either side, was the tree of life, bearing twelve kinds of fruits, yielding its fruit every month, and the leaves of the tree were for the healing of all nations." [1432]

154. This is certainly the River proceeding from the throne of God, that is, the Holy Spirit, Whom he drinks who believes in Christ, as He Himself says: "If any man thirst, let him come to Me and drink. He that believeth on Me, as saith the Scripture, out of his belly shall flow rivers of living water. But this spoke He of the Spirit." [1433] Therefore the river is the Spirit.

155. This, then, is in the throne of God, for the water washes not the throne of God. Then, whatever you may understand by that water, David said not that it was above the throne of God, but above the heavens, for it is written: "Let the waters which are above the heavens praise the Name of the Lord." [1434] Let them praise, he says, not let it praise. For if he had intended us to understand the element of water, he would certainly have said, Let it praise, but by using the plural he intended the Powers to be understood.

156. And what wonder is it if the Holy Spirit is in the throne of God, since the kingdom of God itself is the work of the Holy Spirit, as it is written: "For the kingdom of God is not meat and drink, but righteousness and peace and joy in the Holy Spirit." [1435] And when the Saviour Himself says, "Every kingdom

divided against itself shall be destroyed," [1436] by adding afterwards, "But if I, by the Spirit of God, cast out devils, without doubt the kingdom of God is come upon you," [1437] He shows that the kingdom of God is held undivided by Himself and by the Spirit.

157. But what is more foolish than for any one to deny that the Holy Spirit reigns together with Christ when the Apostle says that even we shall reign together with Christ in the kingdom of Christ: "If we are dead with Him, we shall also live with Him; if we endure, we shall also reign with Him." [1438] But we by adoption, He by power; we by grace, He by nature.

158. The Holy Spirit, therefore, shares in the kingdom with the Father and the Son, and He is of one nature with Them, of one Lordship, and also of one power.

[1432] Rev. xxii. 1, 2.

[1433] S. John vii. 37, 38.

[1434] Ps. cxlviii. 4.

[1435] Rom. xiv. 17.

[1436] S. Matt. xii. 25.

[1437] S. Matt. xii. 27.

[1438] 2 Tim. ii. 11, 12.

Chapter XXI.
Isaiah was sent by the Spirit, and accordingly the same Spirit was seen by him. What is meant by the revolving wheels, and the divers wings, and how since the Spirit is

proclaimed Lord of Sabaoth by the Seraphim, certainly none but impious men can deny Him this title.

159. Since, then, He has a share in the kingdom, what hinders us from understanding that it was the Holy Spirit by Whom Isaiah was sent? For on the authority of Paul we cannot doubt, whose judgment the Evangelist Luke so much approved in the Acts of the Apostles as to write as follows in Paul's words: "Well spake the Holy Spirit through Isaiah the prophet to our fathers, saying: Go to this people and say, Ye shall hear with the ear and shall not understand, and seeing ye shall see and shall not perceive." [1439]

160. It is, then, the Spirit Who sent Isaiah. If the Spirit sent him, it is certainly the Spirit Whom, after Uzziah's death, Isaiah saw, when he said: "I saw the Lord of Sabaoth sitting upon a throne, high and lifted up, and the house was full of His majesty. And the Seraphim stood round about Him, each one had six wings, and with two they were covering His face, and with two they were covering His feet, and with two they were flying; and they cried out one to the other, and said, Holy, holy, holy is the Lord of Sabaoth, the whole earth is full of His majesty." [1440]

161. If the Seraphim were standing, how were they flying? If they were flying, how were they standing? If we cannot understand this, how is it that we want to understand God, Whom we have not seen?

162. But as the prophet saw a wheel running within a wheel [1441] (which certainly does not refer to any appearance to the bodily sight, but to the grace of each Testament; for the life of the saints is polished, and so consistent with itself that later portions agree with the former). The wheel, then, within a

238

wheel is life under the Law, life under grace; inasmuch as Jews are within the Church, the Law is included in grace. For he is within the Church who is a Jew secretly; and circumcision of the heart is a sacrament within the Church. But that Jewry is within the Church of which it is written: "In Jewry is God known;" [1442] therefore as wheel runs within wheel, so in like manner the wings were still, and the wings were flying.

163. In like manner, too, the Seraphim were veiling His face with two wings, and with two were veiling His feet, and with two were flying. For here also is a mystery of spiritual wisdom. Seasons stand, seasons fly; the past stand, the future are flying, and like the wings of the Seraphim, so they veil the face or the feet of God; inasmuch as in God, Who has neither beginning nor end, the whole course of times and seasons, from this knowledge of its beginning and its end, is at rest. So, then, times past and future stand, the present fly. Ask not after the secrets of His beginning or His end, for there is neither. You have the present, but you must praise Him, not question.

164. The Seraphim with unwearied voices praise, and do you question? And certainly when they do this they show us that we must not sometimes question about God, but always praise Him. Therefore the Holy Spirit is also the Lord of Sabaoth. Unless perchance the Teacher Whom Christ chose pleases not the impious, or they can deny that the Holy Spirit is the Lord of powers, Who gives whatever powers He Himself wills.

[1439] Acts xxviii. 25, 26.

[1440] Isa. vi. 1-3.

[1441] Ezek. i. 16.

[1442] Ps. lxxvi. [lxxv] 1.

Chapter XXII.

In proof of the Unity in Trinity the passage of Isaiah which has been cited is considered, and it is shown that there is no difference as to its sense amongst those who expound it of the Father, or of the Son, or of the Spirit. If He Who was crucified was Lord of glory, so, too, is the Holy Spirit equal in all things to the Father and the Son, and the Arians will never be able to diminish His glory.

165. It is now possible to recognize the oneness of the majesty and rule in the Father, the Son, and the Holy Spirit. For many say that it was God the Father Who was seen at that time by Isaiah. Paul says it was the Spirit, and Luke supports him. John the Evangelist refers it to the Son. For thus has he written of the Son: "These things spake Jesus, and departed and hid Himself from them. But though He had done so great signs before them, they did not believe on Him, that the word of Isaiah might be fulfilled which he spake, Lord, who hath believed our report, and to whom hath the Arm of the Lord been revealed? [1443] Therefore, they could not believe, because Isaiah said again, He hath blinded their eyes and hardened their heart, that they might not see with their eyes and understand with their heart and be converted, and I should heal them. [1444] These things said Isaiah when he saw His glory, and spake of Him." [1445]

166. John says that Isaiah spoke these words, and revealed most clearly that the glory of the Son appeared to him. Paul, however, relates that the Spirit said these things. Whence, then, is this difference?

167. There is, indeed, a difference of words, not of meaning. For though they said different things, neither was in error, for both the Father is seen in the Son, Who said, "He that seeth Me seeth the Father also," [1446] and the Son is seen in the Spirit; for as "no man says Lord Jesus, except in the Holy Spirit," [1447] so Christ is seen not by the eye of flesh, but by the grace of the Spirit. Whence, too, the Scripture says: "Rise, thou that sleepest, and arise from the dead, and Christ shall shine upon thee." [1448] And Paul, when he had lost his eyesight, how did he see Christ except in the Spirit? [1449] Wherefore the Lord says: "For to this end I have appeared unto thee, to appoint thee a minister and a witness of the things wherein thou hast seen Me, and of the things wherein thou shalt see Me." [1450] For the prophets also received the Spirit and saw Christ.

168. One, then, is the vision, one the right to command, one the glory. Do we deny that the Holy Spirit is also the Lord of glory when the Lord of glory was crucified who was born from the Holy Spirit of the Virgin Mary? For Christ is not one of two, but is one, and was born as Son of God of the Father before the world; and in the world born as man by taking flesh.

169. And why should I say that, as the Father and the Son, so, too, the Spirit is free from stain and Almighty, for Solomon called Him in Greek pantodunamon, panepischopon , because He is Almighty and beholds all things, [1451] as we showed above to be, [1452] is read in the Book of Wisdom. Therefore the Spirit enjoys honour and glory.

170. Consider now lest perchance something may not beseem Him, or if this displease thee, O Arian, drag Him down from His fellowship with the Father and the Son. But if thou choose

to drag Him down thou wilt see the heavens reversed above thee, for all their strength is from the Spirit. [1453] If thou choose to drag Him down, thou must first lay hands on God, for the Spirit is God. But how wilt thou drag Him down, Who searcheth the deep things of God?

[1443] Isa. liii. 1.

[1444] Isa. vi. 10.

[1445] S. John xii. 36-41.

[1446] S. John xiv. 9.

[1447] 1 Cor. xii. 3.

[1448] Eph. v. 14.

[1449] Acts ix. 8.

[1450] Acts xxvi. 16.

[1451] Wisd. vii. 22.

[1452] B. III. 18.

[1453] Ps. xxxiii. [xxxii.] 6.

15026435R00136

Printed in Great Britain
by Amazon.co.uk, Ltd.,
Marston Gate.